INFORMATION ON
THE RENUNCIATION OF WAR
1927–1928

INFORMATION ON THE
RENUNCIATION OF WAR

1927 ☆ 1928

BY

J. W. WHEELER-BENNETT

WITH AN INTRODUCTION BY

PHILIP H. KERR, C.H., M.A.

KENNIKAT PRESS
Port Washington, N. Y./London

INFORMATION ON THE RENUNCIATION OF WAR

First published in 1928
Reissued in 1973 by Kennikat Press
Library of Congress Catalog Card No.: 72-89272
ISBN 0-8046-1761-9

Manufactured by Taylor Publishing Company   Dallas, Texas

TO

C. R. ("JACK") ACTON

I GRATEFULLY DEDICATE

THIS BOOK

INTRODUCTION

By PHILIP H. KERR, C.H.

THE date when Mr. Kellogg transformed the slow-moving diplomatic exchanges between M. Briand and himself into a proposal addressed by the United States to all the Great Powers that they should renounce war among themselves and undertake to settle international disputes only by pacific means may come to be regarded by history as the real beginning of the end of a system of international intercourse which has deluged Europe in blood every few decades since the fall of the Roman Empire. The essence of that system has been that the nations—and, before the nations, the kings—have regarded war as a rightful, or at least as an inevitable, method of settling their political disputes. So strong was the hold of that fatal concept on men's minds that at the end of the World War of 1914–18, when the statesmen and the peoples made the greatest concerted effort to create an international system which would prevent war of which history has record, and created the League of Nations, they still left war as the *ultima ratio*, the legitimate means which nations could lawfully employ if the pacific procedure of the Covenant failed to produce agreement within some nine months from the outbreak of a dispute.

The Peace Pact, in the main the outcome of the Outlawry of War Movement which originated in the United States, is based upon the repudiation of that concept. It brings the nations into line on the basis that war—that is, the use of violence in its most barbarous, unjust, destructive and inhuman form—can never be a legitimate "institution" to which they can legally and rightfully have recourse as the ultimate method of settling their disputes, and that they must "delegalize" or "outlaw" it altogether and substitute pacific means in its place. In embodying this true idea in a solemn treaty the Great Powers are taking a step towards the prevention of war and the maintenance of permanent peace essentially different from any they have ever previously attempted, for they are setting out to create an international system based upon the same principle as that which alone has maintained peace in any civilized country at any time.

The Peace—the Pax Romana, the Pax Britannica, the Pax Americana and so forth—the peace which we all take for granted inside our own States, is the result of three leading ideas. The first is that the use of violence by any citizen or any group of citizens as the means of settling their disputes or of accomplishing anything is totally renounced and prohibited. The second is that alternative modes of settlement are created —the law courts and the legislatures—whereby every dispute or every social or political problem can be settled by an appeal to reason and justice and not by the will of the physically stronger side. The third is that the police, and if need be the army and the whole citizenry, stand behind the law as security that violence shall not prevail and that pacific means shall be employed. The political philosophy behind the Peace Pact is exactly the same, for it is only by giving effect to these ideas that war can or will ever be outlawed in the world.

The Peace Pact, of course, is only a beginning. It provides for the renunciation of war and the substitution of pacific means in its place. But it does not create the alternative pacific modes of settlement, and it does not give security that States who would try to take the law into their own hands shall be prevented from using war successfully as the instrument of their national policies. The League of Nations, on the other hand, maintains an admirable machinery for the pacific settlement of international disputes by the Court of International Justice, by arbitration, or by investigation, report, and conciliation by the Council or Assembly of the League. It also provides for sanctions against the law-breakers, though in forms which have not gained the confident support of all of its members.

The signing of the Peace Pact does not mean that the United States has decided to join the League of Nations, though its ratification will mean that she will commence to consider afresh her relation to those organizations for the promotion of international peace from which she turned away in 1920. But it means that for the first time all the great Powers, and practically all the smaller Powers, have united in a common undertaking to renounce war and to find alternative methods of settling their disputes. That is a great moral advance, for just in proportion as the nations gain confidence that they are not liable to be called to the arbitrament of war, it will become both easier and more necessary for them to create and employ methods of international settlement in which reason and justice and not the will of the stronger are the deciding factors, and to carry the verdict so arrived at into practical effect. The Peace Pact and the Covenant, while they do not create a world Pax, together embody the fundamental ideas upon which that Pax can be gradually worked out if the public opinion of the leading nations demands it. There is good reason, therefore, for thinking that posterity may regard April 13, 1928, as a turning-point in the history of the world, and will appreciate the enterprise of Mr. Wheeler-Bennett in preparing so accurate and complete a record of the documents and events which have led up to acceptance of the Peace Pact by the United States and by the leading Powers of the League of Nations.

PREFACE

THIS book has for its object the provision of a form of reference to the history of the Kellogg proposals for the renunciation of war which President Coolidge has described as "one of the most impressive peace movements the world has ever seen." It consists of a collection of all the documents relative to the negotiations, with an historical introduction.

I am greatly indebted to His Majesty's Stationery Office for their kind permission to reprint the British White Papers, Cmds. 3109 and 3153 (United States, Nos. 1 and 2, 1928), and to the Committee of Management of the Information Service on International Affairs for allowing me to make use in the historical introduction of material which had appeared in the form of articles in the *Bulletin of International News*.

My grateful thanks are due to my assistant, Mr. Stephen A. Heald, upon whom has fallen much of the work of compiling the documentary section of the book; and I am highly appreciative of the kindness of the various Embassies, Legations, and Dominion Offices which have co-operated most helpfully in supplying the necessary documents.

Finally, I wish to express my sincere thanks to the staffs of the Royal Institute of International Affairs and of the Information Service on International Affairs for the valuable assistance which they have rendered me in the preparation of the book.

J. W. WHEELER-BENNETT

CONTENTS

APPENDIXES

THE HISTORY OF THE
PEACE PACT

THE FIRST PHASE

FRANCO-AMERICAN NEGOTIATIONS

On April 6, 1927, the tenth anniversary of the entry of the United States of America into the World War, M. Aristide Briand, French Foreign Minister, in a statement to the Press,[1] declared that "France would be willing to subscribe publicly with the United States to any mutual engagement tending to outlaw war, to use an American expression, as between these two countries," and thus ushered in the first phase in the negotiations for what has been described as the "greatest step towards world peace since the Covenant of the League of Nations."

In the following June M. Briand embodied his declaration in a draft treaty which was presented by M. Claudel, the French Ambassador, to the Department of State.[2] This draft envisaged a solemn declaration by the two Powers condemning recourse to war, renouncing war as an instrument of national policy, and agreeing that a settlement of all disputes arising between them should be brought about only by pacific means.

Though no official reply was made by the United States Secretary of State for six months after the receipt of this draft, the greatest public interest was evinced in America in M. Briand's declarations throughout the summer and autumn. Three draft treaties were prepared by Professors Shotwell and Chamberlain, the American Foundation and the American Arbitration Crusade respectively, and President Nicholas Murray Butler, through the Carnegie Endowment for International Peace, took the lead in harnessing public opinion towards some method of influencing the action of the Administration. At the same time Mr. S. O. Levinson, Chairman of the American Outlawry of War Committee, visited Paris and conferred with M. Briand. Coincident with these efforts came the great publicity given in the Press to the proposed American Peace Doctrine, put forward by Mr. Wickham Steed, that America

[1] See Document No. I, p. 69.   [2] See Document No. II, p. 72.

should declare its "abhorrence of aggressive war, and that it will never weaken the hands of other nations which may bind themselves together for the purpose of deterring an aggressor or of compelling him to desist from aggression."

Meanwhile, at Geneva, the Eighth Assembly of the League of Nations, representing some fifty-four States, passed unanimously on the morning of September 24th a Resolution declaring—

(1) "That all wars of aggression are, and shall always be, prohibited.

(2) "That all pacific means must be employed to settle disputes of every description which may arise between States."

The Assembly declared that "the States Members of the League are under an obligation to conform to these principles."

With the reassembling of Congress, events began to move more quickly. Public opinion was first voiced officially by Senator Capper, who on November 23rd declared his intention of introducing a Resolution into the Senate that it be declared to be the policy of the United States—

(1) "By treaty with France and other like-minded nations formally to renounce war as an instrument of public policy, and to adjust and settle its international disputes by mediation, arbitration, and conciliation; and

(2) "By formal declaration to accept the definition of aggressor as one which, having agreed to submit international differences to conciliation, arbitration or judicial settlement, begins hostilities without having done so; and

(3) "By treaty with France and other like-minded nations to declare that the nationals of the contracting Governments should not be protected by their Governments in giving aid and comfort to an aggressor nation."

Contemporary opinion in Washington considered that none of the plans for the advancement of the cause of peace outlined by Senator Capper had any chance of favourable action by Congress, and it was generally supposed that President Coolidge and Senator Borah were agreed in thinking the Capper Resolution impracticable.

Mr. Kellogg's reply, which was dated December 28th,[1] but

---

[1] See Document No. III, p. 74.

was not published until January 5, 1928, was in the nature of a wholly different proposal, to the effect that, in contradistinction to the French suggestion of a bi-lateral treaty, an equivalent multi-lateral treaty should be worked out, "thus extending throughout the world the benefits of a covenant originally suggested as between France and the United States alone."

Mr. Kellogg suggested that "the two Governments, instead of contenting themselves with a bi-lateral declaration of the nature suggested by M. Briand, might make a more signal contribution to world peace by joining in an effort to obtain the adherence of all of the principal Powers of the world to a declaration renouncing war as an instrument of national policy." He further said that if the French Government was prepared to assist in such a plan for a multi-lateral treaty, he would be "happy to engage at once on conversations looking to the preparation of a draft treaty following the lines submitted by M. Briand, for submission by France and the United States jointly to the other nations of the world." At the same time the Foreign Offices of the principal Powers were informed of Mr. Kellogg's suggestion.

Objection to the American counter-proposals was at once taken in the French Press. It was pointed out that the adoption of such a formula renouncing *all* war would automatically entail the revision of the whole post-war treaty system of Europe, which was based upon Article 16 of the Covenant of the League of Nations, which definitely envisages the use of armed force as the ultimate deterrent of a covenant-breaking State. Moreover, from the particular viewpoint of France, it was said, such a policy would at once nullify the Locarno Agreement and the guarantees given by France to Poland and Czecho-Slovakia. No multi-lateral agreement to outlaw war could be efficacious without a system of sanctions, and these in themselves entailed the use of armed force. It was one thing to agree to outlaw war between two nations, but quite another to renounce the right to go to war in any and every event.

In his reply, dated January 3rd[1] (made public five days later), M. Briand took up an attitude, which he maintained throughout, that no State such as France, a member of the League of Nations and a party to a variety of treaties of guarantee (in particular the Locarno Agreement), could allow itself the same liberty of action in negotiating a multi-lateral treaty for the outlawry of *all* war as in concluding a bi-lateral agreement with a State not a member of the League and with whom there was, in effect, little chance of war arising. He further pointed out that the Eighth Assembly had already adopted a resolution condemning and prohibiting aggressive war. M. Briand, therefore, declared the willingness of the French Government to concert with that of the United States "in submitting for the approval of all nations an agreement which should be signed beforehand by France and the United States, and by the terms of which the high contracting parties should bind themselves to refrain from any war of aggression, and should declare that they would have recourse for the settlement of disputes of whatever nature which may arise between them to all possible pacific means." This, however, went no farther than the Outlawry of War resolution passed by the Assembly at Geneva in September, 1927.

The reception of M. Briand's reply in America was not a warm one. The American Press attacked it from a variety of angles : that it was a new attempt to inveigle the United States into European politics; that it was a definite commitment (an action always feared by Congress); that the French object was to reserve the right of declaring war on the United States if the "assembled conscience of the world" should declare her to be an aggressor, as, for instance, in the case of Nicaragua. The main objection in American official circles was to the absence of any plan for determining the aggressor State, and there was no inclination to adopt that suggested by Senator Capper, which in turn had been borrowed in a slightly altered form from the Geneva Protocol of 1924.

In his reply, handed on January 11th[2] to M. Claudel for

---

[1] See Document No. IV, p. 76.   [2] See Document No. V, p. 78.

transmission to the Quai d'Orsay, Mr. Kellogg took categorical exception to practically every point raised in M. Briand's Note of January 3rd. He objected to the signing of an outlawry of war pact between the United States and France before submitting it to the Powers, on the grounds that it "might for some reason be unacceptable to one or other of the Great Powers," and he pressed for preliminary discussions with the various Foreign Offices for the purpose of "agreement as to the language to be used." Mr. Kellogg further pointed out that M. Briand's proposal to limit the scope of the pact to the outlawry of aggressive war was a change of front from the original French proposal which "envisaged unqualified renunciation of all war as an instrument of national policy."

The French Press took up at once this statement of Mr. Kellogg's in no uncertain manner, one journal declaring—

"*Lorsque M. Briand avait parlé en juin dernier de la guerre considérée comme instrument de politique nationale, il s'agissait d'un pacte bilatéral entre deux nations qui n'avaient aucune raison de se combattre. Avec un pact plurilatéral, les données du problème ne sont plus les mêmes. La question a été resolue à Genève qui a prohibé la guerre d'agression, et a sanctionné cette prohibition par l'assistance donnée à la puissance attaquée.*"

Nor was criticism confined to the Continental Press. On January 12th the *New York World*, the chief Democrat newspaper of the United States, attacked Mr. Kellogg's proposal as "a masterpiece of ignorance about the nature of the present-day European system. A more accurate description of this proposal would have been to call it a treaty to renounce the Covenant of the League of Nations, the Treaty of Locarno, and all French defensive alliances in Europe."

Finally, the American Note expressed the hope that M. Briand's reservation as to aggressive war was "of no particular significance," and did not represent the last word of the French Government on the subject. The Note urged that the original French draft and the whole of the ensuing correspondence should be forwarded to the Foreign Offices of the Great Powers for their information.

The American attitude of dislike of attempting to define and determine "aggressor" and "aggression" approximates very closely to that of the British Government. This was abundantly evidenced by Mr. Kellogg in a public *exposé* of his policy before the Council on Foreign Relations in New York on March 15th, in which he quoted Sir Austen Chamberlain on the subject.[1] Mr. Kellogg said: "The danger inherent in every definition is recognized by the British Government, which, in a memorandum recently submitted to the subcommittee on Security of the Preparatory Commission on Disarmament of the League of Nations, discussed attempted definition of this character, and quoted from a speech by the British Foreign Secretary in which Sir Austen said: 'I therefore remain opposed to this attempt to define the aggressor because I believe that it will be a trap for the innocent and a signpost for the guilty.' I agree with Sir Austen on this point."

The French reply was prepared for immediate dispatch on January 13th, but on consideration was withheld until after the Cabinet Council of January 17th, and was not presented until the 21st.[2] In it M. Briand defended the action of his Government against the accusation in Mr. Kellogg's Note of a "change of front." He gave official expression to opinions which had already appeared in the French Press, reiterating his earnest desire to co-operate to the full with the United States proposals, but indicating the complexity and difficulties confronting the proposed multi-lateral negotiations and the danger of the resulting pact's being at variance with the provisions of the Covenant of the League and of the other international agreements to which France and the other Great Powers were parties, "all of which engagements impose upon them duties which they cannot contravene."

He maintained that the French proposal of January 5th, to restrict the scope of the proposed pact to the outlawry of *aggressive* war, was an attempt to reconcile the American thesis with that of the League, and was "inspired by a formula which has gained the unanimous adherence of all States Members of

[1] See Document No. VIII, p. 89.   [2] See Document No. VI, p. 82.

the League of Nations, and which for that very reason might be accepted by them with regard to the United States, just as it has already been accepted among themselves."

Thus matters stood at the opening of the Pan-American Conference at Havana on February 16th, which before it closed passed two resolutions relative to the outlawry of war.[1] The first of these contained the statement that "the American Republics desire to express that they condemn war as an instrument of national policy in their mutual relations"; the second resolution declared that "war of aggression constitutes an international crime against the human species," and that "all aggression is considered illicit, and as such is declared prohibited." In his Note of February 27th[2] Mr. Kellogg did not fail to draw the attention of the French Government to the unanimous adoption of these two resolutions by twenty-one American Republics, seventeen of which were States Members of the League of Nations.

In further discussing the difficulties raised by M. Briand with regard to French membership of the League of Nations and participation in existing treaties of guarantee, Mr. Kellogg could not follow the arguments of the French Government. He admitted his inability to understand why the obligations of membership of the League should permit a bi-lateral treaty for the renunciation of war and prohibit a multi-lateral treaty for the same purpose. "It seems to me," he stated in his speech before the Council on Foreign Relations, "that the difference between the bi-lateral and multi-lateral form of treaty, having for its object the unqualified renunciation of war, was one of degree and not of substance, and that a Government able to conclude a bi-lateral treaty would be no less able to become a party to an identical multi-lateral treaty, since it could hardly be presumed that members of the League of Nations were in a position to do separately something that they could not do together." The Note continued that it was

---

[1] See *Bulletin of International News*, published by the Information Service on International Affairs, vol. iv, No. 20, pp. 5–6.

[2] See Document No. VII, p. 85.

idle to continue the discussion of negotiating either bi-lateral or multi-lateral treaties for the renunciation of war if the obligations of the Covenant prevented members of the League from reaching agreement with the United States.

The most important item of the American Note was its unequivocal statement that

"the Government of the United States desires to see the institution of war abolished, and stands ready to conclude with the French, British, Italian, German and Japanese Governments a single multi-lateral treaty, open to subsequent adherence by one or all other Governments, binding the Parties thereto not to resort to war with one another."

Senator Borah, Chairman of the Senate Committee on Foreign Relations, expressed identical views in a statement to the *New York Times* (March 3rd). He declared that unless the League of Nations were organized for war instead of peace the proposed multi-lateral treaty to outlaw war could not possibly conflict with the Covenant. The real obstacle to the multi-lateral treaty was the ten or twelve special alliances which had sprung up in Europe since the World War and were now supported by military conventions.

Senator Borah had also declared that one important result of the proposed treaty

"would be to enlist the support of the United States in co-operative action against any nation which is guilty of flagrant violation of this outlawing agreement. Of course, the Government of the United States must reserve the right to decide in the first place whether or not the treaty has been violated, and secondly what coercive measures it feels obliged to take. But it is quite inconceivable that this country would stand idly by in case of a gross breach of a multi-lateral treaty to which it is a party."

M. Briand, before sending his reply to Washington, took advantage of the meeting of the Council of the League of Nations to discuss the question at length with his colleagues on the Council and with the members of the League Secretariat. It became clear that the European Powers and Japan attached the greatest importance to the American proposals and were anxious to give every chance of success to a suggestion which would secure the active participation of the United States in the preservation of world peace. At the same time they felt it equally essential to safeguard the implication of the Covenant of the League, supplemented by the Locarno Agreement, though France was more than a little concerned as to the fate of the Eastern and Central European treaties of guarantee to which she was a party.

When the text of the French Note was made public on March 31st,[1] these two conflicting policies were evident. M. Briand conceded a point on the inclusion within the province of the proposed pact of all wars, and not merely those of aggression, but laid down the four following reservations, which expressed adequately the French opinion:—

First, that all countries adhere to the treaty, and that the treaty does not become effective until universal adherence is given, unless some special agreement is entered into waiving certain abstentions.

Second, that each country retains the right of legitimate defence.

Third, that in case one country violates its pledge not to engage in war, all others would automatically be released.

Fourth, that the new treaty is not to interfere in any way with the previous obligations of France under the League of Nations, the Locarno agreements, or her neutrality treaties.

Later, on April 17th, the French and United States Governments agreed to submit the entire correspondence which had passed between them relative to a multi-lateral pact for the outlawry of war to the Foreign Offices in London, Berlin, Rome, and Tokio. This agreement definitely both closed the first and opened the second phase of the negotiations.

[1] See Document No. IX, p. 95.

THE United States Government made no direct reply to the French Note of March 31st, but on April 13th it communicated to the British, German, Italian and Japanese Governments a draft treaty, together with a covering note setting forth the official American view thereon.[1] This draft was a brief and concise document of three Articles only; by the first the contracting parties condemn "recourse to war for the solution of international controversies and renounce it as an instrument of national policy in their relations with one another." Article II contained the agreement that "the settlement or solution of all disputes or conflicts of whatever nature or of whatever origin they may be which may arise among them shall never be sought except by pacific means"; the third Article merely provided for ratifications and other technical details. It will be noticed that the wording of the American draft treaty is, *mutatis mutandis*, identical with that of M. Briand's original draft for a Franco-American bi-lateral agreement. The four Governments to whom the draft was circulated were invited to send their observations on it to Washington.

The French Government seems not to have been best pleased that the American draft should have been communicated entirely without consultation with the Quai d'Orsay, considering that it had been Mr. Kellogg's original suggestion that the proposal for a multi-lateral pact should be made under the joint auspices of the two Governments, and further, that it should have ignored all of the reservations contained in the French Note of March 31st. Although hampered by indisposition and the distraction of a General Election campaign, M. Briand at once set about preparing a draft treaty which should place before the four Powers in question the French viewpoint omitted from the American text.

The French Press emphasized, and was at some pains to reiterate later, that the preparation of a second draft was in no way a counter-proposal to that of the United States Govern-

[1] See Document No. X, p. 101.

ment, but was rather intended to provide ground for discussion on which a third and final draft might be based. The draft itself was published on April 21st.[1] Article I declared for the renunciation of war "as an instrument of personal, spontaneous, independent political action . . . and not as an action in which they find themselves involved by an application of a treaty such as the League of Nations." Article II corresponded with the second article of the American draft, but Article III stipulated that if any of the contracting parties contravened the treaty, the others would be absolved from their engagements regarding that party. Article IV laid it down that the stipulations of the present treaty did not affect the rights and obligations resulting from any anterior international acts in which the parties had taken part; and the fifth Article provided that the treaty should have no obligatory force until it had been accepted by all the Powers, unless the signatories to it agreed that it should be put into force in spite of certain abstentions.

Once again Mr. Kellogg made no formal reply to the French point of view, but on April 29th, before the American International Law Association and in the presence of M. Claudel, the French Ambassador, he dealt publicly with the reservations contained in M. Briand's Note of March 31st and in the French draft treaty.[2] As regards the French view safeguarding the right of legitimate defence and of free action in the case of a treaty-breaking State, Mr. Kellogg said that these were self-evident facts; there was nothing in the American draft to impair these rights, and therefore it was unnecessary to include them in the text. By this statement, it may be said that he believed that if nations live up to their obligations to renounce war, the necessity for sanctions will never arise. If, on the other hand, a nation breaks its obligation not to use war as an instrument of national policy, it automatically renounces its rights under the proposed treaty, so that everybody is legally free to take whatever action against it they like. The Secretary of State further declared that in his opinion there was nothing inconsistent between the League Covenant and the idea of the

[1] See Document No. XI, p. 103. [2] See Document No. XII, p. 107.

unqualified renunciation of war. "The Covenant can, it is true, be construed as authorizing war in certain circumstances, but its authorization is not a positive requirement."

This last statement is of the utmost importance and merits consideration. Under the Covenant of the League of Nations possible recourse to war falls into two categories: First, war as a League action authorized by the Council; and secondly, as a potential final settlement of disputes when all other pacific means have failed. With regard to the first, the Council is empowered under at least two separate Articles to take action which might envisage recourse to war. Under Article 10 members of the League incur a liability to respect and preserve each other's territorial integrity against aggression :—

"In case of any such aggression . . . the Council shall advise upon the means by which this obligation shall be fulfilled."

Mr. Kellogg, in his speeches before both the Council on Foreign Relations and the American International Law Association, called attention to the fact that the Fourth Assembly of the League had had submitted to it the following interpretation of this Article :—

"It is for the constitutional authorities of each member to decide, in reference to the obligation of preserving the independence and the integrity of the territory of members, in what degree the member is bound to assure the execution of this obligation."

He added, however, that the Assembly had failed to adopt this interpretation because of one adverse vote.

Again, under Article 16, in the event of a State resorting to war in violation of previous Articles of the Covenant,

"It shall be the duty of the Council in such case to recommend to the several Governments concerned what effective military, naval and air force the members of the League shall severally contribute to the armed forces to be used to protect the Covenant of the League."

It was this obligation in League membership which for some time caused grave concern to Germany, and an interpretation of it formed an important part of the Locarno

Agreement. The contracting parties, other than Germany, assured the latter that, although they could not speak for the League as a whole, they had agreed amongst themselves upon the following interpretation of Article 16:—

". . . the obligations resulting from the said article on the members of the League must be understood to mean that each State member of the League is bound to co-operate loyally and effectively in support of the Covenant and in resistance to any act of aggression to an extent which is compatible with its military situation and takes its geographical position into account."

In the case of what may be called recourse to private war, this is envisaged under paragraph 7 of Article 15, by which a dispute may be dealt with by the Council or the Assembly by the method of conciliation :—

"If the Council fails to reach a report which is unanimously agreed to by the members thereof, other than the representatives of one or more of the parties to the dispute, the members of the League reserve to themselves the right to take such action as they shall consider necessary for the maintenance of right and justice."

The renunciation of all war would therefore perform that action of closing the "gap in the Covenant" which was attempted by the Geneva Protocol of 1924.

In addition to these provisions within the Covenant, there is at least one important international instrument which gives authority to the Council of the League to decide for a recourse to arms, and binds four of the original parties to the multi-lateral treaty. This agreement is the Convention relating to the régime of the Straits, an integral part of the Lausanne Peace Treaty. Article 18 of this Convention guarantees the security of the freedom of the Straits as follows:—

"Should the freedom of navigation of the Straits or the security of the demilitarized zones be imperilled by a violation of the provisions relating to freedom of passage, or by a surprise attack or some act of war or threat of war, the High Contracting Parties (there are eight of them), and *in any case* France, Great Britain, Italy and Japan, acting in conjunction, will meet such a violation, attack or other act of war, or threat of war, by all the means which the Council of the League of Nations may decide for this purpose."

It is probable that considerations of this character were in the mind of M. Briand when he drafted his reservation relating to the obligations of League membership; similarly with that relative to the Locarno Agreement. The Western Pact and the Rhineland Guarantee would indeed be strengthened by the adoption of the American draft, as Mr. Kellogg had indicated, since the High Contracting Parties would in each case (with the exception of Belgium) be identical. But the French Government were exercised in their minds as to the fate of the Eastern Pact, to which Germany, Poland and Czecho-Slovakia are parties, with the guarantee of security by France to the two latter. In the event of Czecho-Slovakia and Poland not adhering to the new Peace Pact, France might be placed in the invidious position of deciding to which of her international obligations she would adhere and from which depart. Hence the reservations regarding the inviolability of the Locarno Agreement.

That Mr. Kellogg fully appreciated this feeling on the part of France is shown by the statement contained in his speech of April 29th. "The United States," he declared, "is entirely willing that all parties to Locarno should become parties to its proposed anti-war treaty, either through signature or by immediate accession to the treaty as soon as it comes into force in the manner provided in Article III of the American draft, and it will offer no objections when and if such a suggestion is made."

It is perhaps particularly the obligations incurred by the treaties which France concluded with Germany's neighbours and others during the period 1920–26, which influenced M. Briand in making his reservations regarding the non-violation of treaties concluded prior to the Outlawry of War Pact and the universal nature of such a pact. These treaties (with Belgium in 1920 and Poland in 1921, and later with Czecho-Slovakia in 1924 and Rumania and Yugo-Slavia in 1926)[1] have always been looked upon with suspicion in Washington—and, indeed in other countries—and regarded as an

[1] See Wheeler-Bennett and Langerman, *Information on the Problem of Security*, George Allen & Unwin, 1927, pp. 40–4, 194, 198.

indication that the French were "playing safe" in trusting both to the new diplomacy of the League of Nations and the old pre-war system of alliances. The French view, however, is that these agreements were negotiated as a substitute for the security against future German aggression assured to France by the Anglo-American guarantee of June 28, 1919, which had never become operative on account of the refusal of the United States Senate to ratify the Versailles Treaty, upon which it was made dependent.

Against this view it may be said that with the exception of the French guarantee to Poland and Czecho-Slovakia under the Eastern Pact already referred to, the remaining agreements, as far as they were concluded for the guarantee of French security, have been superseded by the Locarno Agreement, and it was Mr. Kellogg's suggestion that France should secure the early adherence of those States, to whom her guarantee is promised, to the anti-war pact proposed by the United States.

In dealing with the French reservation on the universality of the treaty Mr. Kellogg said:—

"From a practical standpoint, it is clearly preferable, however, not to postpone the coming into force of the anti-war treaty until all the nations of the world can agree on the text of such a treaty and cause it to be ratified. For one reason or another States so situated as to be no menace to the peace of the world might obstruct an agreement or delay ratification in such a manner as to render abortive the efforts of all other Powers."

"It is highly improbable, moreover, that the form of the treaty acceptable to the British, French, German, Italian, and Japanese Governments, as well as to that of the United States, would not equally be acceptable to most, if not all, of the other Powers of the world. Even if this were not the case, however, the coming into force among the above-named six Powers of an effective anti-war treaty and the observance thereof would be a practical guarantee against a second world war.

"This in itself would be a tremendous service to humanity, and the United States is unwilling to jeopardize the practical success of the proposal which it has made by conditioning the coming into force of the treaty upon prior universal acceptance or almost universal acceptance."

Of the four recipients of the American Note of April 13th, Dr. Stresemann secured a strategic score for Germany by being first in the field, on April 27th, with an unqualified acceptance of Mr. Kellogg's proposals, the basic ideas of which he declared to be in accordance with the principles of German policy.[1] The proposed pact, Dr. Stresemann thought, would not be in conflict either with the principles of the League Covenant and the Locarno Agreement or with Germany's existing obligations apart from these. The latter consist principally of the Soviet-German treaty of non-aggression signed in April 1926, by which the two parties are pledged to preserve a benevolent neutrality towards one another in the event of one being the victim of aggression by a third party.

There is little doubt that the confirmation contained in the German Note, both of his own proposals and of his views on the French reservations, influenced Mr. Kellogg very considerably in the drafting of his speech before the American International Law Association two days later. Further support for the American point of view as opposed to the French arrived on May 9th with the reply of the Italian Government, in which Signor Mussolini declared that Italy welcomed the American initiative with lively sympathy and offered his cordial co-operation towards agreement.[2]

It was, however, for the British reply that Washington anxiously waited. Mr. Kellogg had been at some pains to demonstrate his desire to meet the British point of view, as shown by his adoption of the British Government's attitude towards the definition of aggression, and there was evidence to show that Britain's peculiar position in relation to France was realized and appreciated in Washington. Of public opinion in England there was little doubt, since prominent politicians publicly welcomed the American proposals, and bodies, both religious and secular, passed resolutions endorsing them. Official opinion, however, was bound to take into consideration both the geographical propinquity of Great Britain to Europe and the psychological distance from it of her own natural feelings and those of the Dominions.

Sir Austen Chamberlain's first reaction on the receipt of the

[1] See Document No. XIII, p. 111.   [2] See Document No. XIV, p. 114.

American and French draft treaties was to suggest the reference
of both to a conference of Jurists, and by this means, which
had proved so valuable in reconciling the rival drafts prepared
in connection with the Locarno Agreement, to aid in the
reduction to a minimum of all possible differences as regards
the wording of the pact. In view, however, of the unfavourable
reception of this suggestion in Washington, it was withdrawn,
and in a statement made to the House of Commons on May 10th
the Foreign Secretary explained the Government's delay in
replying to the American Note, first, because of the necessity
of consulting the Dominions, as the Government was particularly anxious that the policy of the whole Empire should be
at one in the matter; and secondly, because he was desirous
that every party in the negotiations should have ample time
to realize the full import the implications involved. "It is
necessary to get a document which all can sign in the same
spirit, which all can sign meaning the same thing, which all
can sign with the same good will, the same heartiness and the
same determination to maintain it."[1]

Sir Austen's speech was interpreted by both the French and
American Press as endorsing their respective points of view,
but a further elucidation of both official and public opinion was
provided on May 15th, when the House of Lords, in an act
almost unprecedented in history, adopted unanimously, without
the formality of a division, a motion by Lord Reading:—

"That this House cordially welcomes the proposals of the United
States Government for renunciation of war, and, whilst recognizing
the desire of His Majesty's Government to co-operate in securing the
peace of the world, is of opinion that prompt and favourable consideration should be given to these proposals, and that His Majesty's Government should declare their acceptance of their principles embodied in
the proposed treaties to the United States Government."[2]

When the British Note of reply was finally handed to Mr.
Houghton, the American Ambassador, on May 19th,[3] it was
found to be a reasoned statement of view, going deeply into

---

[1] Hansard (House of Commons), May 10th, p. 458.
[2] Hansard (House of Lords), May 15th, p. 14.
[3] See Document No. XV, p. 115.

the basic principles of the pact and developing the points of similarity rather than of divergency in the American and French draft treaties. The British Government stated its conviction that there was no serious divergency in effect between the proposals of the two Governments, and that it was understood that there would be no objection to the modification suggested by M. Briand that there was no intention in the pact preventing the parties to the Covenant and the Locarno Agreement from fulfilling their obligations.

With the aim of the United States Government "to embody in a treaty a broad statement of principle, to proclaim without restriction or qualification that war shall not be used as an instrument of policy," the British Government declared themselves "wholly in accord." The French proposals "had merely added an indication of certain exceptional circumstances in which the violation of that principle by one party may oblige the others to take action seeming at first sight to be inconsistent with the terms of the proposed pact."

The Note contained one particular paragraph of vital importance:—

"The language of Article I, as to the renunciation of war as an instrument of national policy, renders it desirable that I should remind your Excellency that there are certain regions of the world the welfare and integrity of which constitute a special and vital interest for our peace and safety. His Majesty's Government have been at pains to make it clear in the past that interference with these regions cannot be suffered. Their protection against attack is to the British Empire a measure of self-defence. It must be clearly understood that His Majesty's Government in Great Britain accept the new treaty upon the distinct understanding that it does not prejudice their freedom of action in this respect. The Government of the United States have comparable interests any disregard of which by a foreign Power they have declared that they would regard as an unfriendly act. His Majesty's Government believe, therefore, that in defining their position they are expressing the intention and meaning of the United States Government."

Sir Austen Chamberlain concluded by saying that the British Dominions were all "in cordial agreement with the general principles of the proposed treaty," and would be prepared, on receipt of an invitation, to participate with His

Majesty's Government in Great Britain in the conclusion of such a treaty.

Mr. Kellogg was not slow to avail himself of this suggestion, for on May 22nd[1] Mr. Houghton presented to Sir Austen Chamberlain a Note extending through him "to His Majesty's Governments in Australia, New Zealand and South Africa, and to the Government of India, a cordial invitation in the name of the Government of the United States to become original parties to the treaty for the renunciation of war." On the same day a similar invitation was conveyed to Canada and the Irish Free State in identic Notes presented by the American Ministers in Ottawa and Dublin.[2]

In some circles in Washington there was a little anxiety as to whether the mention in the British Note of "certain regions," which was understood to refer to British obligations in regard to Egypt, might not influence Japan to make a similar reservation in respect of her special interest in Manchuria. There was at the time considerable activity of Japanese troops in that province on account of the uncertain fate of Pekin and the determination of the Tokio Government to prevent the Chinese civil war from spreading over an area in which much good Japanese labour and capital had been spent. It was even rumoured that Japan meditated declaring a protectorate over Manchuria on the analogy of Great Britain's action in Egypt in December 1914.

When, however, the Japanese reply was handed to Mr. McVeagh by Baron Tanaka, on May 26th,[3] it was found to contain no such reservation, but rather an expression of warm sympathy with the American proposals, which, it was understood, contained nothing to prejudice the right of a State to self-defence or to the fulfilment of obligations under the Covenant and the Locarno treaties. The Japanese Government expressed its firm belief that "unanimous agreement on a mutually acceptable text for such a treaty as is contemplated is well capable of realization by discussion between the six

[1] See Document No. XVII, p. 122.   [2] See Document No. XVIII. p. 124.
[3] See Document No. XVI, p. 120.

Powers referred to," and the cordial co-operation of Japan was promised to secure this end.

It was not only in regard to possible Japanese imitation that a certain trepidation was felt in certain quarters as to the paragraph of Sir Austen's Note of May 19th embodying the British reservation. Though both the Irish Free State[1] and Canada[2] made cordial replies of acceptance on May 30th to the American Note of May 22nd, discussions on the issues raised by the British reservation as to "certain regions of the world the welfare and integrity of which constitute a special and vital interest for our peace and safety" occurred in Parliament, both in Dublin and Ottawa.

In the Dail on May 31st Mr. de Valera complained, firstly, that the American invitation had come at the instance of Great Britain and not directly from Washington; and secondly, that the British reservation implied "a right on the part of Britain to say that wherever British interests, wherever British Imperialism is affected, wherever they have interests, that they have a right to use war, that that right should be recognized by us and by every other signatory to this proposed pact, that the right of the British to use war as an instrument of their national policy in any part of the world . . . in any region where their interests can be affected, shall be recognized." He declared himself opposed to the British reservation on the same grounds that he had opposed Article 10 of the Covenant of the League of Nations, "because it would be a recognition of the right of the British to hold Ireland and interfere in Egypt, to hold India and interfere in China."

In replying, Mr. McGilligan, Minister for External Affairs, explained that the invitation had come to the Free State Government from the United States Government through the usual diplomatic channels. "We were not invited originally with the United States, France, Japan, Italy and Germany. Why? Because we are not one of the six great Powers. That is why the invitation did not issue to us in the first instance. . . . If there is anything with regard to the late period at which it

---

[1] See Document No. XIX, p. 126.   [2] See Document No. XX, p. 127.

came, the fact that it has come to us at all directly is an advance." As regards the British reservation, Mr. McGilligan drew the attention of the Dail to the final paragraph of Sir Austen's Note, which opens with the statement that "the detailed arguments in the foregoing paragraphs are expressed on behalf of His Majesty's Government in Great Britain." "These arguments," said Mr. McGilligan, "have no application to us whatever."[1]

Similarly, on June 7th, in the Canadian House of Commons, Mr. Garland, of the Progressive Party, asked the Prime Minister "whether, because of the obvious commitments and moral obligations implied in the reservation made by Sir Austen Chamberlain, he would agree in the first place that the Canadian Parliament should have an opportunity of discussing the treaty before ratification; and secondly, whether he would give the House a statement about his acceptance or otherwise of Sir Austen Chamberlain's reservations."

Mr. Mackenzie King's reply was very similar to that of Mr. McGilligan. "Sir Austen Chamberlain," he said, "was speaking with respect to the British Government and announcing its policy. The British Government is free to pursue whatever course it wishes with respect to signing. It may have reservations which it will wish and has a perfect right to make." He added that the Canadian Government was not called upon to express its views upon Sir Austen's reservations.[2]

The replies of the remainder of the Dominions Governments —that is to say, those affected by Mr. Houghton's Note of May 24th—made almost uniform expression of acceptance; New Zealand on May 30th,[3] Australia on June 2nd,[4] the Government of India on June 12th,[5] and South Africa on June 15th.[6] Of these South Africa was the most guarded in that it stated that the Union Government took it for granted, in accepting the American invitation, that the proposed pact would not deprive any party of its rights of legitimate self-defence; that violation

---

[1] Official Report of the debate in the Dail, May 31st, pp. 2482–2491.
[2] See *The Times*, June 8, 1928.   [3] See Document No. XXI, p. 130.
[4] See Document No. XXII, p. 131.   [5] See Document No. XXIII, p. 132.
[6] See Document No. XXIV, p. 133.

by one party freed all the others from their obligations; and
that by becoming a party to the proposed pact South Africa
would not be precluded from fulfilling her obligations as a
member of the League of Nations.

Meanwhile, the period during which the replies to the American invitation were coming in was utilized on both sides of the
Atlantic for a further clarification of official attitudes. The first
step in this direction was taken by President Coolidge, who
made his first official pronouncement on the Kellogg proposals
in the course of his address on the battlefield of Gettysburg
on Memorial Day, May 30th.[1] He described the proposals as
"one of the most impressive peace movements that the world
has ever seen," and declared it to be his "earnest hope that
the ideals which have inspired the French Minister for Foreign
Affairs and the Secretary of State of the United States in their
joint efforts to find a solution of the problem of peace may find
a practical realization in the early making of a multi-lateral
treaty limiting future resort to war." This speech had the
important effect of showing clearly upon which side the
President stood, and did much to dispel the impression, current
in certain quarters, that the proposals were the child of the
Secretary of State alone and had not the support of the Chief
Executive.

In the course of his journey to Geneva Sir Austen Chamberlain discussed with M. Briand the outstanding subjects of
mutual interest between them, and on June 2nd a statement
was issued from the Quai d'Orsay which added slightly to the
elucidation of the Franco-British attitude towards the Kellogg
proposals. In answer to a question as to the present stage of
the negotiations, M. Briand replied, *"On est tangent à la réussite,"*
and justified his optimism in the following words:—

"It was indispensable that we should be quite sure that the pact
would not contain anything conflicting with obligations contracted
by members of the League of Nations and the signatories of the Locarno
Treaties. It was necessary to reserve the right of legitimate defence.
It was necessary to give the pact the widest possible character of uni-

[1] See Document No. XXV, p. 135.

versality. It was further necessary to specify that an infraction of the pact by one of the contracting parties restored to all the others their liberty of action. This was the purpose of the reservations put forward by the French Government. The negotiations have shown that all these reservations have been accepted by the other Powers, and that Mr. Kellogg has recognized that our concern for them was justified. The ground has thus been cleared. It is now only necessary to search for a formula, and France will certainly put no obstacle in the way of finding one. Mr. Kellogg wants it to be simple, clear-cut and striking. I am convinced that something of this nature will soon be discovered. An agreement will be reached, and this time it will be perfectly plain."[1]

On June 11th Mr. Kellogg brought the second phase of the negotiations to a close in the course of a speech delivered in the Hotel Pennsylvania, New York, on the occasion of the tercentenary of the founding on American soil of the first church of the Dutch Reformed Faith. The speech of the Secretary of State showed clearly his satisfaction at the reception with which his proposals had met in Europe, and was interpreted as an indication that he was not prepared to issue an amended text of his first draft treaty. With a certain subtlety he gave full justice to M. Briand for initiating the negotiations, which, he pointed out, were to perpetuate peace and not war. His final statement summed up the attitude of the American administration:—

"I am persuaded that the time has come when a frank renunciation of war as an instrument of national policy should be made, to the end that the peaceful and friendly relations now existing between the peoples of the world may be perpetuated. I am convinced, moreover, that all changes in these relations should be sought only by pacific means, and be the result of a peaceful and orderly process; and any nation which shall hereafter seek to promote its national interests by resort to war should be denied the benefits and guarantees furnished by the proposed treaty. This is the object of the negotiations in which fifteen world Powers are now engaged, and in the name of the Government of the United States I bespeak the continued support of this and every other Church in the present movement for the promotion of world peace."[2]

Further evidence of the whole-hearted support with which Mr. Kellogg's proposals met in his own party was given on June 13th, when the Republican National Convention at

[1] See *The Times*, June 4, 1928.   [2] See Document No. XXVI, p. 137.

Kansas City, Missouri, having nominated Mr. Hoover as their candidate for the forthcoming Presidential Election, gave formal ratification to the plan for the renunciation of war by incorporating it as a plank in the party platform in the following words :—

"We endorse the proposal of the Secretary of State for a multilateral treaty, proposed to the principal Powers of the world, and open to signature by all nations, to renounce war as an instrument of national policy, and declaring in favour of the pacific settlement of international disputes. The idea has stirred the conscience of mankind and gained widespread approval both of Governments and of the people, and the conclusion of the treaty will be acclaimed as the greatest single step in history towards the conservation of peace."[1]

[1] See *The Times*, June 15, 1928.

ON Saturday , June 23rd, the American diplomatic representatives in fourteen capital cities presented identic Notes covering a third draft treaty at the respective Foreign Offices.[1] Thus in one step Mr. Kellogg had increased the number of negotiating States by three and had opened the third phase of the negotiations.

The extension of the sphere of negotiations to include the three minor Locarno Powers, Belgium, Czecho-Slovakia and Poland, was not unexpected. Mr. Kellogg had expressed his willingness to do this in his speech before the American International Law Association, and it had been known for some time that diplomatic conversations had been in progress between the Department of State, the Belgian Embassy, and the Czecho-Slovak and Polish Legations. Moreover, Dr. Beneš's visit to Paris and London at the end of May had been in this connection.

The text of the articles of the treaty remained identical with that of the first American draft circulated on April 13th, but modifications were made in the preamble to meet the views of both the British and French Governments. The paragraph in the first draft reading:—

"Inspired by a common desire not only to perpetuate the peaceful and friendly relations now happily subsisting between their peoples, but also to prevent war among any of the nations of the world,"

was omitted from the new preamble, and a new paragraph was inserted as follows:—

"Convinced that all changes in their relations with one another should be sought only by pacific means and be the result of a peaceful and orderly process, and that any signatory Power which shall hereafter seek to promote its national interests by resort to war should be denied the benefits furnished by this treaty."

Thus, by extending the number of original contracting parties to include all the signatories to the Locarno Agreement, and by inserting in his revised preamble a definite statement

[1] See Document No. XXVII, p. 141.

that any deliberate infraction of peace by one State automatically released all other signatories from their obligations towards it, Mr. Kellogg had gone far to meet the majority of the original French reservations. It was intended that the provisions of the League Covenant and of Locarno and of France's other post-war agreements, of the inviolability of which M. Briand had been so jealous, should be safeguarded completely, and could be brought at once into operation against any aggressor State.

The covering Note in tone closely resembled Mr. Kellogg's speech before the American International Law Association, from which it quoted freely and extensively. Of particularly vital importance was the following passage dealing with self-defence:—

"There is nothing in the American draft of an anti-war treaty which restricts or impairs in any way the right of self-defence. That right is inherent in every sovereign State and is implicit in every treaty. Every nation is free at all times, and regardless of treaty provisions, to defend its territories from attack or invasion, and it alone is competent to decide whether circumstances require recourse to war in self-defence. If it has a good case, the world will applaud and not condemn its action. Express recognition by treaty of this inalienable right, however, gives rise to the same difficulty encountered in any effort to define aggression. It is the identical question approached from the other side. In this respect, no treaty provision can add to the natural right of self-defence. It is not in the interest of peace that a treaty should stipulate a juristic conception of self-defence, since it is far too easy for the unscrupulous to mould events to accord with an agreed definition."

The Note disclosed the attitude of the United States Government as being "satisfied that the draft treaty proposed by it on April 13, 1928, could be properly accepted by the Powers of the world without change" except as regards the inclusion of the British Dominions and the minor Locarno Powers. The Government had, however, "no desire to delay or complicate the present negotiations by rigidly adhering to the precise phraseology of that draft, particularly since it appears that, by modifying the draft in form, though not in substance, the points raised by other Governments can be satisfactorily met."

The Note further declared that the United States Government would be prepared to have "included among the original signatories the parties to the neutrality treaties referred to by the Government of the French Republic, although it believes that the interests of those States would be adequately safeguarded if, instead of signing in the first instance, they should choose to adhere to the treaty." From this it would be gathered that, though as yet uninvited and unmentioned in the list of contracting parties in the first paragraph of the preamble, Rumania and the Serb-Croat-Slovene State would, should they express a wish to do so, become original signatories.

Perhaps the most important passages of the Note were those in which the American Government declared its readiness to sign at once a treaty in the form proposed, and invited the other contracting parties to make statements "at as early a date as may be convenient" whether they were prepared to do likewise.

For a period of three weeks after the receipt of Mr. Kellogg's Note no official statement on it was made by any of the recipients, although continuous negotiations were in progress between the various Foreign Offices. Occasion was taken in both the British and French Press to draw attention to the fact that although the new American draft had made concessions to the French reservations, these had been embodied only in the revised preamble, and Mr. Kellogg had himself stated in his address before the Council on Foreign Relations, on March 15th, that "a preamble is not a binding part of a treaty," and it was felt that if this were so, a loophole was left by which some signatory Power might find itself unable to discharge its obligations under the Covenant of the League of Nations.

The Quai d'Orsay at once submitted the draft treaty to its legal experts, and the opinions of the leading jurists of the other negotiating Powers were also sought. In addition, M. Philippe Berthelot, Secretary-General of the Quai d'Orsay, paid a flying visit to London to "feel the pulse" of the British

Foreign Office. It was the desire of M. Briand to obtain the embodiment in the agreement of some more definite recognition of the safeguarding of the rights and obligations of France (and, of course, of the other negotiating Powers), under the Covenant and the Locarno Treaties, than that implied in the preamble. The suggestion was therefore put forward that a special protocol should be annexed to the proposed treaty, and should be signed concurrently with it by all parties. Thus, while not altering Mr. Kellogg's draft text, the French reservations would be formally placed on record on the same terms of equality with the American formula.

M. Briand's feelings were reflected clearly in the attitude of the Belgian Foreign Office towards the pact. M. Paul Hymans, speaking in the Chamber of Deputies on July 6th, while expressing his warmest sympathies for the American proposals, added:—

> "*Mais je tiens a marquer aussitôt la nécessité de maintenir intégralement le Pacte de la Société des Nations et le Traité de Locarno, qui constituent les bases de notre status international et les garanties de nos sécurités.*"

In Germany there was no hesitancy nor had the change of Government altered the friendly attitude of that country towards the pact. Herr Hermann Müller, the Socialist Chancellor, in reading his programme of policy to the Reichstag on July 3rd, declared that his Government "would do everything possible to further that great conception." This statement was elaborated in the German reply to Mr. Kellogg which Herr Schubert dispatched on July 11th (made public on July 13th),[1] thereby maintaining Germany's record of being the first in the field with an unqualified concurrence with the interpretation contained in the American draft of the Covenant and the Locarno Treaty, and a definite acceptance of Mr. Kellogg's invitation to sign the pact as it stood, without further reservation. It is important to note that the German reply was not made without reference to the other Powers, since *The Times* of July 13th stated that it had only been dispatched after

[1] See Document No. XXVIII, p. 150.

a conference at Berlin between Sir Cecil Hurst, M. Fromageot, and Dr. Gaus, the legal advisers to the British, French, and German Foreign Offices, who were in agreement that the interpretation of the proposed pact, contained in Mr. Kellogg's covering Note of June 23rd, covered almost every possible eventuality. The absence of the Italian legal expert from this conference may be explained by reference to Signor Mussolini's original answer to Mr. Kellogg's first circular Note of April 15th, in which the Italian Government stated that "in its opinion such a meeting (of international jurists) can only be effective if the participation of a legal expert of the Government of the United States is assured."

When the French reply, which was handed to Mr. Herrick on July 14th, was made public on July 17th,[1] it was found, to the relief of many who believed that any addition to the text of the agreement would prejudice the United States Senate against it, that all suggestion of an annexed protocol had been abandoned, and that M. Briand, in accordance with the verdict of the conference of legal experts, had accepted the interpretation of the treaty contained in Mr. Kellogg's Note of June 23rd. The Note recapitulated the original French reservations, which, it agreed, were covered by the American interpretation referred to and by the revised preamble. Moreover, the invitation by Mr. Kellogg to all the Locarno Powers and to those other States who are party to French treaties of neutrality, to be original signatories of the pact, provided "that character of generality which accords with the views of the French Government." Therefore—

"In view of the provisions of the new preamble and the interpretation given to the treaty, the French Government finds that the new convention is compatible with the obligations to which France is a contracting party. In these circumstances the French Government is happy to be able to declare to the Government of the United States that it is now ready to sign the treaty."

The silence maintained by the British Government as to the nature of their reply to Mr. Kellogg's Note gave rise to some

[1] See Document No. XXIX, p. 151.

anxiety and criticism in certain pacifist quarters. At a meeting of the National Peace Congress at the Caxton Hall on July 6th Lord Cecil made the following statement:—

"I do venture to think that the continued delay is unfortunate, and that we have really now had quite enough time to consider whether we are going to say 'Yes' or 'No' to these proposals—and to hope before many days, or weeks, at any rate, that we shall have said 'Yes' without reservation."

He added significantly that the great majority of the people of this country were in earnest about renunciation, disarmament and arbitration: "They mean to have it done, if not by this Government by some other."

On the following day Sir Austen Chamberlain was closely questioned in the House of Commons by Mr. Thurtle. In a brief but able defence of his policy the Foreign Secretary said that it was "more important that His Majesty's Government should be careful when undertaking new engagements not to break their old ones than to proceed without reference to the serious nature of the questions involved." Four days later (July 11th) in reply to further questions on the same subject, Sir Austen explained that his consultations with the Dominion Governments and with the Government of India were in process, and that he confidently hoped to be able to dispatch the British reply before the end of the Parliamentary session. He took full responsibility for the delay involved in replying, "but," he added, "I use the word 'delay' to signify the time taken in the careful consideration of the proposal."

This line of argument was followed up on July 14th by the Home Secretary, Sir William Joynson-Hicks, who stated at a Conservative rally near Evesham: "It has been said that we were not so keen on that pact as other nations, but that is absolutely untrue. In the last few weeks His Majesty's Government have been giving particular care to the proposals of the United States of America, and when our reply has been settled by the Cabinet we shall find that we are not in the least bit behind France or Germany in our enthusiastic acceptance of the idea of the outlawry of war." He added that "it is no use

signing a pact with a pen unless you sign it with the heart,"
and demonstrated that the Kellogg proposals must be the
prelude to international reduction of armaments. In conclusion he said: "We desire to appeal to the great United
States, when our signature, in the course of a few weeks, is
placed alongside that of the other nations of Europe, and
say to them:—

" 'We are signing the pact at your request, a pact to end war, and
yet we understand that you are increasing your Navy.' "

Finally, Sir Austen Chamberlain announced in the House
of Commons on July 16th that the British reply would be
handed to the American Chargé d'Affaires on the 18th. This
was accordingly done, and Sir Austen, in informing the House
of the fact, declared that the British Government would be
happy to sign the treaty "at such time and place as may be
agreeable to the Government of the United States." On the
same evening the Secretary of State for War, Sir Laming
Worthington-Evans, speaking at a Conservative meeting in the
country, declared that Great Britain and the Dominions had
accepted with alacrity the American proposals. "We were
delighted," he continued, "that the movement had come from
the United States, for we regarded it as a matter of the most
supreme importance that America should not dissociate from
Europe or from the main duties of assisting to preserve the
peace of Europe and of the world."

The text of the British Note was published on July 20th as
a White Paper (Cmd. No. 3153).[1] Therein Sir Austen Chamberlain accepted the explanations and interpretation of the
American draft treaty, which had formed the main part of
Mr. Kellogg's Note of June 23rd. He also agreed that the
revised preamble was "sufficient to meet" the point at issue
over the safeguarding of the execution of Great Britain's
obligations as a member of the League of Nations. Sir Austen
expressed satisfaction at the inclusion of all the Locarno Powers
as original signatories to the Pact. As it was most desirable

---

[1] See Document No. XXX, p. 153.

and also the wish of the United States that all States should adhere to the pact, he hoped "that a general invitation will be extended to them to do so."

The Foreign Secretary reiterated his statement of May 19th that His Majesty's Government accepted the treaty on the strict understanding that its provisions did not impair the Government's freedom of action in "certain regions of which the welfare and integrity constitute a special and vital interest for our peace and safety." He concluded with the declaration that

"His Majesty's Government in Great Britain are glad to join with the Government of the United States and with all other Governments similarly disposed in signing a definitive treaty for the renunciation of war in the form transmitted in your Note of June 23rd. They rejoice to be associated with the Government of the United States of America and the other parties to the proposed treaty in a further and signal advance in the outlawry of war."

Of the British Dominions, the Irish Free State was the first to accept the American proposals on July 14th,[1] while the acceptances of the Australian, New Zealand, and South African Governments and of the Government of India[2] were handed to the American Chargé d'Affaires with the British Note. The Canadian Government also replied on July 18th.[3]

The Italian reply, the nature of which was, it is assumed, arrived at without previous consultation with other contracting Powers, was handed to Mr. Fletcher, the American Ambassador in Rome, on July 15th,[4] and consisted of the following brief statement:—

"The Royal Government, which has carefully examined the draft treaty for the outlawry of war proposed by the United States, takes cognizance of and agrees with the interpretation given by the United States to the same treaty in its Note of June 23rd, and with such premises declares itself willing to sign."

The Belgian[5] and Polish[6] Notes of reply, embodying unqualified acceptance of the proposals, were handed to the

[1] See Document No. XXX, p. 153. [2] See Document No. XXXV, p. 161.
[3] See Document No. XXXVI, p. 165. [4] See Document No. XXXI, p. 154.
[5] See Document No. XXXII, p. 155. [6] See Document No. XXXIII, p. 156.

American Ministers in Brussels and Warsaw on July 17th, and the Japanese[1] and Czecho-Slovak[2] Governments dispatched similar Notes on July 20th.

A further addition to the number of States, now amounting to sixteen, invited to be original signatories of the Peace Pact was made on July 14th, when General Primo de Riviera, Marques de Estella, communicated to his Cabinet an invitation from Mr. Kellogg to Spain to participate, "couched in the most friendly terms."

[1] See Document No. XXXVIII, p. 169.
[2] See Document No. XXXVII, p. 166.

With the receipt of the last acceptances, those of Japan and Czecho-Slovakia, on July 20th, the third phase of the negotiations may be said to have closed, and the fourth opened a week later (July 27th), when M. Briand began to issue invitations for the formal signing of the pact in Paris on August 27th.

In England there had been considerable criticism of what was termed the dilatory policy adopted by the Foreign Secretary, and this found vent during the debate in the House of Commons on the Foreign Office Vote on July 30th, when the Opposition speakers found fault both with his delay in replying and with the British reservation. Sir Austen Chamberlain in his reply dealt faithfully with his critics, pointing out to them that in the earlier stages of the negotiations Mr. Kellogg had taken six months to reply to M. Briand; he (Sir Austen) had taken five weeks to reply to Mr. Kellogg. Mr. Kellogg took six weeks to reply to him, and he took between three and four weeks to send his final reply to Mr. Kellogg. He reiterated his statements made on July 8th and 11th, that due consideration had had to be taken of the effect of the acceptance of the Kellogg proposals upon Great Britain's League of Nations and Locarno obligations. With regard to the reservation, "that British doctrine which is the equivalent of the Monroe Doctrine of the United States," Sir Austen asked his critics if they really believed that in making their proposals the American Government had meant to abolish or change their singular policy in regard to the Monroe Doctrine. "Why should it be thought that this country is doing something unreasonable or which might wreck the whole scheme if it stated, what we all know to be true, that there are certain parts of the world in which we, too, have a Monroe Doctrine?"

He was under no delusion as to what the pact might bring about. "I do not want great expectations to be followed by great deceptions." He concluded with the important statement that he believed that the real efficacy of the pact depended

"not on any engagement taken by the United States Government, but on how the rest of the world thought the United States are going to judge the action of an aggressor, and whether they will help him or hinder him in his aggression. If the American nation ranges itself behind its own treaty, then, indeed, the signature of its treaty will be an additional detriment to war, and it will be, in addition, the most valuable security for peace."

As far as Great Britain was concerned, the seal of approval of the acceptance of the Kellogg proposals was set by the following passage from the King's Speech on the Prorogation of Parliament on August 3rd:—

"My Government have been happy to accept the proposed treaty for the renunciation of war in the form in which it was finally proposed to them by the Government of the United States. The proposed treaty has similarly been accepted by my Governments in the Dominions and by the Government of India. It is my confident expectation that, when completed, it will constitute a new and important guarantee of the world's peace."

On the following day, August 4th, the British Foreign Office forwarded to the Secretary-General of the League at Geneva copies of the two British Notes of May 19th and July 18th, which had been sent in reply to Mr. Kellogg's circulation of his first and second draft treaties. In their covering Note the Foreign Office gave the following reason for this step:—

"In considering these proposals, His Majesty's Government in Great Britain have been at great pains, in view of the provisions of Article 20 of the Covenant of the League of Nations, to assure themselves that their acceptance would not involve any inconsistency with the obligations resulting from the Covenant. As appears from the enclosed Notes, they are satisfied that signature of the proposed treaty will not involve any conflict with the obligations resulting from membership of the League. As the matter is evidently one of general interest to all the members of the League, I am to request that copies of the enclosed Notes may be circulated to them."

It was at this moment, just when the procedure for the official ceremony in Paris was in process of arrangement by the Quai d'Orsay, that the spectre at the feast arose. Some of the warmest supporters of Mr. Kellogg's proposals had felt that without the inclusion of Russia the pact for the outlawry of war would be no more than a "loud-sounding nothing," as

Metternich had described the Holy Alliance. As early as May 18th the subject had been raised by General Smuts, who, in an interview given to the Cape Town correspondent of *The Times*, while fully approving the spirit and principle of the pact, gave this warning:—

"It seems to me that it is essential that Russia should also become a signatory to the declaration. It would be vain to organize world peace and leave out Russia."

He added that he believed that Russia would be "only too anxious to be associated with the declaration, even if, like the United States, she will not become a member of the League."

As the course of the negotiations proceeded and the intention of widening the scope of the pact was developed, it was felt by many that if the Baltic States were to become signatories, and if the pact itself was to be the prelude to a general reduction of armaments, the inclusion of Russia was absolutely essential. This school of opinion made itself heard both at "question-time" on July 30th and in the Foreign Office debate which followed. Mr. Noel Buxton elicited from Sir Austen the information that in the event of an invitation being sent to the Soviet Government he would neither support it nor oppose it, and both Mr. Lloyd George and Mr. Arthur Ponsonby returned to the subject in the debate. The first declared that "I think it is vital, if you are going to condemn war and make war impossible, that somehow or other you should bring Russia within the ambit of some obligation not to make war. You will never get disarmament until you do that." Mr. Ponsonby was more positive. "I believe," he said, "that if Soviet Russia is invited to sign the pact the invitation will be accepted gladly. . . . I believe it most important, at the moment, that Russia should be brought in."

Hard on this came a statement by M. Chicherin, Soviet Commissar for Foreign Affairs, issued from Moscow on August 5th. This declared that the Kellogg proposals were merely a new manifestation of the anti-Soviet policy which, it was alleged, had been pursued by the capitalist Powers since the Locarno

Agreement in 1925. The statement ended with a challenge to the Powers to disprove their hostile intentions towards Russia:—

"If the Powers wish the participation of the U.S.S.R. they can still send an invitation. The Soviet Government would accept such an invitation. If it is not sent, it will be an admission by the Powers that the pact is directed against the U.S.S.R."

The Spanish Government also claimed the right of being a party to the original signature of the pact, by virtue of the invitation extended to Spain by Mr. Kellogg on July 14th to become a contracting party. After some colloquy between the Quai d'Orsay and the Department of State it was decided that official invitations to the ceremony of signature at Paris on August 27th should be issued to those Powers (fourteen in all) who were recipients of Mr. Kellogg's final Note on June 23rd, but that the Treaty would be open for signature by all States immediately after the original contracting parties had signed it.

It was further announced from the State Department that although the ceremony of signing would take place in Paris, the deposit of ratifications would be made at Washington, the honours being thus shared between the two initiatory Powers. This would, of course, mean that in the event of the U.S.S.R.'s signing the Treaty, her ratifications would have to be deposited at Washington through the agency of some other signatory Power having diplomatic relations both with the U.S.S.R. and with America, since the latter country has recognized no Government in Russia since that of Kerensky.

As the date for the final signing of the pact drew on, general regret was felt on all sides that the illness of Sir Austen Chamberlain would prohibit him from signing an agreement in the framing of which he had played a distinguished rôle. It was felt, too, that it was unfortunate that a document of such great political and international importance as the Peace Pact should not be signed by His Majesty's Principal Secretary of State for Foreign Affairs. Lord Cushendun, the Acting Foreign Secretary, however, gave general satisfaction by his letter to the Archbishop of Canterbury on August 20th.

The arrival of the United States Secretary of State and the Canadian Prime Minister at Havre on August 24th was the signal for a further manifestation of Franco-American amiabilities. Mr. Kellogg was hailed by the mayor as the "Artificer of Peace" and presented with a gold pen, inscribed with laurel wreaths and bearing the legend: "*Si vis pacem, para pacem.*" Mr. Kellogg himself gave the final assurance of the intended universality of the pact, which now began to be known by its official title of *Traité Général pour la Renonciation à la Guerre,* in a statement given to the Press on Saturday, August 25th:—

"We are here," he said, "to sign a Treaty in which I hope all other nations will join, thus taking a great step forward in the interests of world peace. It was the grand conception of M. Briand which was the origin of this historic treaty."

On the afternoon of Monday, August 27th, therefore, the plenipotentiaries of fifteen Powers met at the Quai d'Orsay to sign the General Treaty for the Renunciation of War, and the mere fact of their presence there together was an indication of the progress that had been made towards international co-operation. In particular, the visit of Herr Stresemann was significant, since it was the first time since prior to the war of 1870 that a German Foreign Minister had been received officially at the Quai d'Orsay. The Salle de l'Horloge, in which exactly ten years ago the principal nations of the world had accepted the Covenant of the League of Nations, was crowded with diplomats, Cabinet Ministers, and representatives of the Press. Great arc lights had been installed to facilitate the cinematographing of the ceremony, and on the head of the horseshoe table at which the delegates sat a microphone and broadcasting apparatus had been installed.

The ceremony itself was of the simplest. Apart from an eloquent address such as M. Briand can always be counted upon to make on such occasions, there was no speech-making. Each in his turn, the fourteen statesmen advanced to a smaller table and signed the Treaty, embossed upon parchment, using Mr. Kellogg's presentation gold pen and the inkstand which more than a century and a half before, in 1775, had been used to sign the first Franco-American Treaty between the already moribund French Monarchy and the struggling infant American Republic.

The ceremonies commenced at three o'clock, M. Briand's speech, its translation and the formal reading of the pact in French and English occupying some forty-five minutes. The actual signing began at 3.45 p.m., Lord Cushendun acting as signatory both for Great Britain and the Crown Colonies and for the Government of India. The whole ceremony was over by four o'clock.

Immediately after the conclusion of the ceremony of sig-nature the Quai d'Orsay issued an official *communiqué* declaring the Treaty open to the adherence of all States. On the same day American diplomatic representatives in the capitals of all States of the world which were not original Contracting Parties, with the exception of the U.S.S.R. and Afghanistan, presented a circular Note inviting their adherence to the pact.[1] In the Note the United States Government recapitulated at some length the course of the negotiations and at the same time communicated the official text of the pact.[2] As a result of this some 31 States have registered with the State Department at Washington their willingness to adhere.[3]

The duty of inviting the adherence of the U.S.S.R. devolved upon the French Government as being the only one of the two initiatory Powers to have diplomatic relations with Moscow. Accordingly, on August 27th, M. Herbette, French Ambassador, made a verbal invitation to M. Maxim Litvinov, Acting Commissar for Foreign Affairs, during the absence on sick-leave of M. Chicherin. He subsequently communicated a com-plete *dossier* of the official correspondence which had passed between the Powers previous to the signing of the pact, and also an official text. The Soviet reply[4] was dated August 31st, and in it M. Litvinov expressed the willingness of his Govern-

---

[1] See Document No. XL, p. 178.   [2] See Document No. XLII, p. 188.
[3] For a complete list to date of States which have adhered to the pact see p. 192.   [4] See Document No. XLI, p. 181.

ment to adhere. In a long and somewhat rambling argument he criticized the absence of any provision in the pact for the reduction or limitation of armaments and declared that the only logical corollary was the universal acceptance of the plans for disarmament which had been put forward by the Soviet Representative on the Preparatory Disarmament Commission of the League of Nations. M. Litvinov further criticized the system of making reservations to the pact, but said that as these reservations, more particularly the British, had been accepted by all signatory and adhering Powers, it should be expressly stated precisely what was implied by them, and in the case of the British reservations just what "regions of the world" were referred to. The main point, however, of the Soviet Reply was acceptance of the pact and presumably all it implied.

The Pact of Paris, as was to be expected, formed one of the principal topics of reference in the speeches made during the early plenary sessions of the Ninth Assembly of the League of Nations, which opened at Geneva on September 3rd. M. Voldemaras, the Lithuanian Prime Minister, proposed a draft resolution on September 8th which envisaged the amendment of the Covenant in view of the acceptance of the pact by States Members of the League. The resolution ran as follows :—

"The Assembly,

"Learning with deep emotion that the United States of America and several States Members of the League of Nations signed a pact for the renunciation of war on August 27, 1928, in Paris;

"Noting that several other States Members or non-Members of the League of Nations have already acceded to the said pact;

"Recognizing that the acceptance of the pact for the renunciation of war by the Members of the League of Nations goes further than their obligations in this respect contained in the Covenant of the League of Nations and supplements them, thus necessitating changes in the fundamental provisions of the Covenant of the League of Nations;

"Recalling the Assembly resolution of September 24, 1927, condemning wars of aggression;

"Requests the Council to initiate an inquiry into the amendments which should be introduced into the Covenant of the League of Nations on the above-mentioned lines, and to submit these amendments to the Assembly at its next session."

The Assembly referred this draft resolution to its Agenda Committee, who reported back on September 11th. The Committee were of the opinion that a discussion on the subject of the relations of the pact to the Covenant could not usefully take place during the present session of the Assembly both on account of the fact that the pact had not yet come into force and because "the essential importance and the scope of the problem raised by the draft resolution of M. Voldemaras would necessitate a thorough study, which the delegates of the Governments now sitting in the committees of the Assembly would hardly take up without having the necessary time to ask for and receive instructions from their Governments." The Assembly therefore decided to give up any idea of discussing the Lithuanian resolution. The Lithuanian delegation, however, reserved the right to take the necessary steps to ensure that its proposal should be included in the agenda of the Tenth Assembly.

In effect, the Treaty signed on August 27th condemns war as an instrument of national policy, but with the following qualifications: According to the interpretation placed upon its text in the various Notes exchanged, and which has, accordingly, apparently been agreed upon, recourse to war is permitted

(1) In self-defence.

(2) Against any treaty-breaking signatory State.

(3) In execution of any obligation consequent upon the signing of any treaty of neutrality, or, in the case of Great Britain, in defence of certain places or strategic points which are vital to the safety of the Empire.

(4) In fulfilment of the obligations and responsibilities incurred by membership of the League of Nations and by the signature of the Locarno Agreement.

In M. Briand's eloquent words:—

"For the first time, in face of the whole world, through a solemn covenant involving the honour of great nations that all have behind them a heavy past of political conflicts, war is renounced unreservedly as an instrument of national policy—that is to say, in its most specific and dreaded form: selfish and wilful war."

It is generally accepted that the future of the Pact of Paris depends upon the attitude which the United States Senate decides to adopt towards it. Despite the general feeling of optimism and elation at the ultimate fruition of a seed sown as far back as April 1927, there are already the beginnings of a cloud on the horizon, which though it may not have reached the dimension of a man's hand, is a reminder that a treaty is not operative until it is ratified. More than one representative speaker in the United States has declared his opposition to the pact, and claimed that the Senate will not accept it. Mr. Kellogg, when asked as to the chances of the ratification of the Pact in the forthcoming session in December, permitted himself the somewhat Delphic reply: "It is impossible to say to-day what the American Senate will do to-morrow." On the other hand, Mr. Wickham Steed, writing in the *Sunday Times* of August 26th, declared that

"Unless some of the European signatories of the Peace Pact have been, or should be, guilty of a culpable misreading of the American situation, the Peace Pact is certain to be ratified by the Senate. The movement behind it in the United States is too strong to be withstood."

It is the British reservation which, it is said, will form one of the principal stumbling-blocks to American approval. On this point Senator Borah, upon whose personal attitude much hangs, made an important statement early in September[1]:—

"Some other Senators now in Washington," he said, "are at a loss to understand how letters of interpretation of the pact, such as those that have been written to the American Secretary of State, can be regarded as reservations to the Treaty itself. These interpretations were not embodied in the Treaty before it was signed by the nations, and these Senators take the view that these Governments are bound by what they signed, since in their judgment the language of the Treaty is specific and plain. Unless some statement on this phase of the subject has been made before the next session of Congress, it is likely that the Foreign Relations Committee will make a formal inquiry of the State Department before recommending favourable action by the Senate."

Without incurring the dangers of prophecy, it is safe to say that there is every indication that when the pact comes up

[1] See *The Times*, September 6, 1928.

for discussion in the Senate, it will meet with a certain opposition, the strength and influence of which it is impossible at the present time to estimate. In the meantime, it is of interest to note that the ratifications of the pact are to be deposited and exchanged at Washington, and it is the duty of the United States Government under the Treaty to communicate all news of ratification, adhesion, etc., to the other contracting Powers. The Treaty itself, of course, only comes into operation when the ratifications of all the original signatories have been exchanged, so that the refusal of one Power to ratify may nullify the whole agreement.

The great principle underlying the Pact of Paris may best be summarized in the words with which M. Briand concluded his speech before the final ceremony of signature on August 27th:—

"*Il n'est pas une des nations ici représentées qui n'ait versée son sang sur les champs de bataille de la dernière guerre: je vous propose de dedier aux morts, à tous les morts de la grande guerre, l'évènement que nous allons consacrer de notre signature.*"

PRINCIPAL DATES IN THE HISTORY OF THE PEACE PACT

1927.

April 6. M. Briand issued statement to the Associated Press containing suggestion of the renunciation of war between France and the United States.

June 20. M. Briand submitted proposal of a bi-lateral treaty to Mr. Kellogg.

Dec. 28. Mr. Kellogg replied suggesting a multi-lateral treaty.

1928.

Jan. 5. French Note to Mr. Kellogg limiting renunciation to wars of aggression.

11. American Note to the French Ambassador, M. Paul Claudel.

21. French Note to Mr. Kellogg.

Feb. 27. American Note to the French Ambassador.

Mar. 15. Mr. Kellogg's Address before the Council on Foreign Relations, New York.

26. French Note to Mr. Kellogg containing the French reservations.

April 7. Agreement between France and the United States to submit correspondence on the subject of the Peace Pact to the Foreign Offices of Great Britain, Germany, Italy and Japan, and to invite their views.

13. American Note to the Foreign Ministers of Great Britain, Germany, Italy and Japan enclosing the American Draft Treaty.

21. Publication of the French Draft Treaty.

27. Reply of the German Government to the American Note of April 13, stating its unqualified acceptance.

29. Mr. Kellogg's speech before the American International Law Association replying to the French reservations.

May 9. Reply of the Italian Government.

10. Statement by Sir Austen Chamberlain in the House of Commons.

15. Resolution in favour of the Peace Pact passed unanimously, without a division, in the House of Lords.

18. Statement by General Smuts to *The Times*.

19. Reply of the British Government.

24. Note presented to the Governments of the Irish Free State and Canada by U.S. Ministers in Dublin and Ottawa, inviting them to become parties to the Peace Pact.

24. Note presented to Sir Austen Chamberlain on behalf of the Governments of Australia, New Zealand and South Africa, and the Government of India, inviting them to become parties to the Peace Pact.

26. Reply of the Japanese Government.

30. Reply of the Irish Free State Government.

1928.

May 30. Reply of the New Zealand Government.

30. President Coolidge's Memorial Day speech at Gettysburg, in which he supported the Peace Pact.

June 1. Reply of the Canadian Government.

2. Reply of the Australian Government.

2. Sir Austen Chamberlain and M. Briand, after a conversation in Paris, issued a statement.

11. Mr. Kellogg's speech at the Hotel Pennsylvania, New York.

12. Reply of the Government of India.

14. The Republican National Convention at Kansas City, U.S.A., included endorsement of Mr. Kellogg's proposals as a plank in its platform.

15. Reply of the South African Government.

20. The Foreign Affairs Committee of the French Senate approved the principle of the pact to Outlaw War on condition that it did not interfere with the obligations of States members of the League of Nations.

23. American Note handed to all the Locarno Powers (including Belgium, Czecho-Slovakia and Poland) and the British Dominions, enclosing revised draft of the American Draft Treaty, including concession to French reservations in an additional paragraph in the Preamble.

July 3. Statement of policy with regard to the Peace Pact by Herr Müller, the German Chancellor, in the Reichstag.

5–7. Conference between British, French and German Foreign Office legal experts in Berlin, Sir Cecil Hurst, M. Froma- geot and Dr. Gaus.

6. Statement of policy with regard to the Peace Pact by M. Hymans, Belgian Minister for Foreign Affairs, in the Belgian Chamber.

8. Sir Austen Chamberlain's answer to questions in the House of Commons explaining the delay in the dispatch of the British reply to the American Note of June 23.

11. Sir Austen Chamberlain's replies to questions in the House of Commons assuming full responsibility for delay in dispatch of the British reply.

11. Acceptance of German Government in reply to the American Note of June 23.

11. French Council of Ministers approved the draft of M. Briand's reply to the American Note of June 23.

14. Acceptance of the French Government.

14. American Note to the Spanish Government inviting Spain to become an original signatory to the Peace Pact.

14. Acceptance of the Irish Free State Government.

15. Acceptance of the Italian Government.

17. Acceptance of the Belgian Government.

17. Acceptance of the Polish Government.

1928.

July 18. Acceptance of the Governments of Great Britain, Australia, New Zealand and South Africa and of the Government of India.

18. Acceptance of the Canadian Government.

20. Acceptance of the Czecho-Slovak and Japanese Governments.

27. M. Briand issued invitations for the signing of the pact at Paris on August 27th.

30. Sir Austen Chamberlain, in the course of the debate on the Foreign Office vote in the House of Commons, made a statement on the British attitude towards the pact.

Aug. 3. The King's Speech proroguing Parliament approved the acceptance of the pact.

5. M. Chicherin issued a statement in Moscow to the effect that the U.S.S.R. would accept an invitation to sign the pact if one were extended.

27. Signature in Paris of the General Treaty for the Renunciation of War.

27. U.S. Circular Note presented to all States not original signatories to the pact (except the U.S.S.R. and Afghanistan), inviting their adherence.

27. The French Ambassador in Moscow verbally invited the adherence of the U.S.S.R.

31 The Soviet Government notified its adherence in a Note to the French Ambassador.

DOCUMENTS

RELATIVE TO THE CONCLUSION OF THE PACT FOR THE RENUNCIATION OF WAR

I

STATEMENT TO THE ASSOCIATED PRESS MADE BY M. ARISTIDE BRIAND ON APRIL 6, 1927[1]

A l'heure où la pensée du monde occidental se reporte à cette date solennelle de l'entrée en guerre des Etats-Unis, j'adresse au peuple américain l'expression émue des sentiments très fraternels et très confiants que nourrira toujours pour lui le peuple français.

Je n'oublie pas que c'est à moi que fut réservé d'apprendre, le premier, par une communication officieuse de M. Sharp, alors ambassadeur des Etat-Unis à Paris, que le gouvernement fédéral avait pris la détermination qui devait exercer une influence si considérable dans l'histoire de la guerre mondiale.

Dix années se sont écoulées depuis que la nation américaine, dans un élan magnifique, s'associait aux nations alliées pour la défense des libertés menacées, et au cours de ces années, un même esprit de justice et d'humanité n'a cessé d'animer nos deux pays, également soucieux de mettre fin à la guerre et d'en empêcher le retour.

La France veut autour d'elle une atmosphère de confiance et de paix et ses efforts se sont traduits par la signature d'accords tendent à écarter la menace des conflits. La limitation des armements, recherchée aussi sincèrement par nos deux gouvernements, répond aux vœux ardents du peuple français tout entier, sur qui pèsent depuis plus d'un demi siècle de lourdes charges militaires et qui a supporté pendant quatre ans sur son territoire des dévastations non encore réparées.

Les discussions sur le désarmement ont pu faire apparaître toute la complexité du problème technique soumis à l'examen d'experts, elles ont permis du moins de dégater, politiquement, la communauté d'inspiration et l'identité de buts qui existent entre la France et les Etats-Unis. Deux grandes nations démocratiques, éprises du même idéal de paix, cheminent d'un même pas vers la même conclusion: les divergences de vues qui peuvent se manifester entre elles ne portent jamais

[1] *Le Temps*, April 7, 1927.

que sur des questions de procédure ou de méthode. Et là
même où les propositions de la France ne peuvent rencontrer
celles des Etats-Unis elles établissent du moins clairement
aux yeux du peuple américain combien la France, sous la seule
réserve de sa sécurité, est prête à s'engager loin dans la voie
des réalisations.

Faut-il rappeler les propositions françaises, à Genève,
tendant à limiter la plus redoutable des menaces de guerre
de demain par le contrôle de l'armement industriel et chimique
des Etats? La France a été plus loin encore lorsqu'elle a
proposé l'institution internationale d'un "état-major général de
la paix." Enfin, dans l'organisation de ses forces nationales,
elle donne, en ce moment même, la preuve de son inspiration
éminemment pacifique en envisageant la reconstitution de
son armement d'un point de vue purement défensif. La nouvelle
loi militaire actuellement soumise au Parlement français a
bien été conçue par les hommes les plus hostiles au danger du
militarisme: elle tend pour la première fois à "supprimer la
conception le la guerre profitable" et fait supporter à tous,
hommes ou femmes, le poids abominable de la guerre, le nation
tout entière étant ainsi mise en garde contre un péril commun.
Une telle organisation n'est-elle pas exclusive de toute tendance
agressive ?

Plus que telle ou telle question de procédure dans l'élabora-
tion technique d'un projet de désarmement, c'est cette question
fondamentale d'une politique de paix, c'est-à-dire d'une
volonté de paix et d'un esprit de paix, qui importe vraiment.
Car le désarmement après tout, ne peut résulter que de la
volonté de paix des nations du monde civilisé. Et c'est par là
que la pensée américaine est assurée toujours de rencontrer la
pensée française.

Pour qui s'attache à cette réalité vivante d'une politique
de paix, les Etats-Unis et la France apparaissent déjà dans le
monde comme moralement solidaires. S'il en était besoin,
entre ces deux grandes démocraties, pour témoigner encore
plus hautement en faveur de la paix et proposer aux peuples
un exemple plus solennel, la France serait prête à souscrire

publiquement, avec les Etats-Unis, toute engagement mutuel tendant à mettre entre ces deux pays, suivant l'expression américaine, "le guerre hors la loi." La renonciation à la guerre comme instrument de politique nationale est une conception déjà familière aux signataires du pacte de la Société des Nations et des traités de Locarno. Tout engagement souscrit dans le même esprit, par les Etats-Unis, envers une autre nation comme la France, contribuerait grandement, aux yeux du monde, à élargir et fortifier la base sur laquelle s'édifie une politique internationale de la paix. Ainsi deux grandes nations amies, également dévouées à la cause de la paix, auraient fourni au monde la meilleure illustration de cette vérité que la réalisation la plus immédiate à atteindre n'est pas tant le désarmement que la pratique de la paix.

En souvenir de ce dixième anniversaire de l'entrée en guerre des Etats-Unis, le Légion américaine se prépare à faire un pieux pèlerinage en France, où reposent ses morts et où se tiendra sa convention annuelle. Je souhaite que les légionnaires viennent ici le plus nombreux possible: ils y seront les bienvenus. De leur trop court séjour parmi nous ils emporteront, je le sais, le souvenir d'une France au travail, aussi désireuse de la paix qu'elle a été ardente à la guerre, et largement ouverte à tout ce qu'il-y-a de grand et de généreux qui fait battre les cœurs à l'unisson des vôtres.

II

ENGLISH TRANSLATION OF M. BRIAND'S PROPOSAL SUB-
MITTED TO THE SECRETARY OF STATE OF THE UNITED
STATES ON JUNE 20, 1927[1]

DRAFT OF PACT OF PERPETUAL FRIENDSHIP BETWEEN FRANCE AND THE UNITED STATES

The President of the French Republic and the President of
the United States of America,

Equally desirous of affirming the solidarity of the French
people and the people of the United States of America in their
wish for peace and in their renunciation of a recourse to arms
as an instrument of their policy towards each other,

And having come to an agreement to consecrate in a solemn
act these sentiments, as much in accord with the progress of
modern democracies as with the mutual friendship and esteem
of two nations that no war has ever divided, and which the
defence of liberty and justice has always drawn closer,

Have to this end designated for their plenipotentiaries, to wit,

The President of the French Republic:

The President of the United States of America:

who, after having exchanged their powers, recognized in good
and due form, have agreed upon the following provisions:—

ARTICLE 1.

The high contracting Powers solemnly declare, in the name
of the French people and the people of the United States of
America, that they condemn recourse to war, and renounce it
respectively as an instrument of their national policy towards
each other.

[1] From Command Paper No. 3109, Correspondence with the United States
Ambassador respecting the United States Proposal for the Renunciation of
War (hereinafter referred to as British White Paper), p. 3.

ARTICLE 2.

The settlement or the solution of all disputes or conflicts, of whatever nature or of whatever origin they may be, which may arise between France and the United States of America, shall never be sought by either side except by pacific means.

ARTICLE 3.

The present Act shall be ratified, the ratifications thereof shall be exchanged at   as soon as possible, and from that time it shall have full force and value.

In witness whereof the above-named plenipotentiaries have signed the present Act and have thereunto set their seal.

Done at Paris in two copies (each drawn up both in French and English and having equal force) the   1927.

III

MR. KELLOGG, U.S. SECRETARY OF STATE, TO M. PAUL CLAUDEL,[1] FRENCH AMBASSADOR IN WASHINGTON, DECEMBER 28, 1927

December 28, 1927.

EXCELLENCY,

I have the honour to refer to the form of treaty entitled "Draft of Pact of Perpetual Friendship between France and the United States" which his Excellency the Minister for Foreign Affairs was good enough to transmit to me informally last June through the instrumentality of the American Ambassador at Paris.

This draft treaty proposes that the two Powers should solemnly declare in the name of their respective peoples that they condemn recourse to war, renounce it as an instrument of their national policy towards each other, and agree that a settlement of disputes arising between them, of whatsoever nature or origin they may be, shall never be sought by either party except through pacific means. I have given the most careful consideration to this proposal and take this occasion warmly to reciprocate on behalf of the American people the lofty sentiments of friendship which inspired the French people through his Excellency M. Briand to suggest the proposed treaty.

The Government of the United States welcomes every opportunity for joining with the other Governments of the world in condemning war and pledging anew its faith in arbitration. It is firmly of the opinion that every international endorsement of arbitration and every treaty repudiating the idea of a resort to arms for the settlement of justiciable disputes materially advances the cause of world peace. My views on this subject find a concrete expression in the form of the arbitration treaty which I have proposed in my Note to you of December 28, 1927, to take the place of the Arbitration Convention of 1908. The proposed treaty extends the scope of that convention

---

[1] From British White Paper, Cmd. 3109, p. 4.

and records the unmistakable determination of the two Governments to prevent any breach in the friendly relations which have subsisted between them for so long a period.

In view of the traditional friendship between France and the United States—a friendship which happily is not dependent upon the existence of any formal engagement, and in view of the common desire of the two nations never to resort to arms in the settlement of such controversies as may possibly arise between them, which is recorded in the draft arbitration treaty just referred to—it has occurred to me that the two Governments, instead of contenting themselves with a bi-lateral declaration of the nature suggested by M. Briand, might make a more signal contribution to world peace by joining in an effort to obtain the adherence of all the principal Powers of the world to a declaration renouncing war as an instrument of national policy. Such a declaration, if executed by the principal world Powers, could not but be an impressive example to all the other nations of the world and might conceivably lead such nations to subscribe in their turn to the same instrument, thus perfecting among all the Powers of the world an arrangement heretofore suggested only as between France and the United States.

The Government of the United States is prepared therefore to concert with the Government of France with a view to the conclusion of a treaty among the principal Powers of the world, open to signature by all nations, condemning war and renouncing it as an instrument of national policy in favour of the pacific settlement of international disputes. If the Government of France is willing to join with the Government of the United States in this endeavour, and to enter with the United States and the other principal Powers of the world into an appropriate multi-lateral treaty, I shall be happy to engage at once in conversations looking to the preparation of a draft treaty following the lines suggested by M. Briand for submission by France and the United States jointly to the other nations of the world.

Accept, etc.,

FRANK B. KELLOGG.

IV

M. CLAUDEL TO MR. KELLOGG, JANUARY 5, 1928[1]

On January 5, 1928, the French Ambassador transmitted his Government's reply to the American Note of December 28, 1927, which reads as follows:—

(*Translation.*)

January 5, 1928.

MR. SECRETARY OF STATE,

By a letter of December 28th last your Excellency was kind enough to make known the sentiments of the Government of the United States concerning the suggestion of a treaty proposed by the Government of the Republic in the month of June 1927 with a view to the condemnation of war and the renunciation thereof as an instrument of national policy between France and the United States.

According to your Excellency, the two Governments, instead of limiting themselves to a bi-lateral treaty, would contribute more fully to the peace of the world by uniting their efforts to obtain the adhesion of all the principal Powers of the world to a declaration renouncing war as an instrument of their national policy.

Such a declaration, if it were subscribed to by the principal Powers, could not fail to be an impressive example to all the nations of the world, and might very well lead them to subscribe in their turn to the same pact, thus bringing into effect as among all the nations of the world an arrangement which at first was only suggested as between France and the United States.

The Government of the United States, therefore, would be disposed to join the Government of the Republic with a view to concluding a treaty between the principal Powers of the world which, open to the signature of all nations, would condemn war, would contain a declaration to renounce it as an instrument of national policy, and would substitute therefor the pacific settlement of disputes between nations.

[1] From British White Paper, Cmd. 3109, p. 6.

Your Excellency added that, if the Government of the Republic agrees thus to join the Government of the United States and the other principal Powers of the world in an appropriate multi-lateral treaty, your Excellency would be happy to undertake immediately conversations leading to the elaboration of a draft inspired by the suggestions of M. Briand and destined to be proposed jointly by France and the United States to the other nations of the world.

The Government of the Republic appreciated sincerely the favourable reception given by the Government of the United States to the proposal of M. Briand. It believes that the procedure suggested by your Excellency and carried out in a manner agreeable to public opinion and to the popular sentiment of the different nations would appear to be of such nature as to satisfy the views of the French Government. It would be advantageous immediately to sanction the general character of this procedure by affixing the signatures of France and the United States.

I am authorized to inform you that the Government of the Republic is disposed to join with the Government of the United States in proposing for agreement by all nations a treaty to be signed at the present time by France and the United States and under the terms of which the high contracting parties shall renounce all war of aggression, and shall declare that for the settlement of differences of whatever nature which may arise between them they will employ all pacific means. The high contracting parties will engage to bring this treaty to the attention of all States and invite them to adhere.

The Government of the Republic is convinced that the principles thus proclaimed cannot but be received with gratitude by the entire world, and it does not doubt that the efforts of the two Governments to ensure universal adoption will be crowned with full success.

Accept, etc.,

PAUL CLAUDEL.

V

MR. KELLOGG TO M. CLAUDEL, JANUARY 11, 1928[1]

January 11, 1928.

EXCELLENCY,

In the reply which your Government was good enough to make to my Note of December 28, 1927, his Excellency the Minister for Foreign Affairs summarized briefly the proposal presented by the Government of the United States, and stated that it appeared to be of such a nature as to satisfy the views of the French Government. In these circumstances, he added that the Government of the Republic was disposed to join with the Government of the United States in proposing for acceptance by all nations a treaty, to be signed at the present time by France and the United States, under the terms of which the high contracting parties should renounce all wars of aggression and should declare that they would employ all peaceful means for the settlement of any differences that might arise between them.

The Government of the United States is deeply gratified that the Government of France has seen its way clear to accept in principle its proposal that, instead of the bi-lateral pact originally suggested by M. Briand, there be negotiated among the principal Powers of the world an equivalent multi-lateral treaty open to signature by all nations. There can be no doubt that such a multi-lateral treaty would be a far more effective instrument for the promotion of pacific relations than a mere agreement between France and the United States alone, and if the present efforts of the two Governments achieve ultimate success, they will have made a memorable contribution to the cause of world peace.

While the Government of France and the Government of the United States are now closely in accord so far as the multi-lateral feature of the proposed treaty is concerned, the language of M. Briand's Note of January 5, 1928, is in two respects open to an interpretation not in harmony with the idea which

[1] From British White Paper, Cmd. 3109, p. 7.

the Government of the United States had in mind when it submitted to you the proposition outlined in my Note of December 28, 1927. In the first place, it appears to be the thought of your Government that the proposed multi-lateral treaty be signed in the first instance by France and the United States alone and then submitted to the other Powers for their acceptance. In the opinion of the Government of the United States this procedure is open to the objection that a treaty, even though acceptable to France and the United States, might for some reason be unacceptable to one of the other great Powers. In such event the treaty could not come into force, and the present efforts of France and the United States would be rendered abortive. This unhappy result would not necessarily follow a disagreement as to terminology arising prior to the definitive approval by any Government of a proposed form of treaty, since it is by no means unreasonable to suppose that the views of the Governments concerned could be accommodated through informal preliminary discussions and a text devised which would be acceptable to them all. Both France and the United States are too deeply interested in the success of their endeavours for the advancement of peace to be willing to jeopardize the ultimate accomplishment of their purpose by incurring unnecessary risk of disagreement with the other Powers concerned, and I have no doubt that your Government will be entirely agreeable to joining with the Government of the United States and the Governments of the other Powers concerned for the purpose of reaching a preliminary agreement as to the language to be used in the proposed treaty, thus obviating all danger of confronting the other Powers with a definitive treaty unacceptable to them. As indicated below, the Government of the United States would be pleased if the Government of France would agree that the draft treaty submitted by M. Briand last June should be made the basis of such preliminary discussions.

In the second place, and this point is closely related to what goes before, M. Briand's reply of January 5, 1928, in expressing the willingness of the Government of France to join with the

Government of the United States in proposing a multi-lateral treaty for the renunciation of war, apparently contemplates that the scope of such treaty should be limited to wars of aggression. The form of treaty which your Government submitted to me last June, which was the subject of my Note of December 28, 1927, contained no such qualification or limitation. On the contrary, it provided unequivocally for the renunciation by the high contracting parties of all war as an instrument of national policy in the following terms:—

"Article 1.

"The high contracting Powers solemnly declare, in the name of the French people and the people of the United States of America, that they condemn recourse to war and renounce it respectively as an instrument of their national policy towards each other.

"Article 2.

"The settlement or the solution of all disputes or conflicts, of whatever nature or of whatever origin they may be, which may arise between France and the United States of America, shall never be sought by either side except by pacific means."

I am not informed of the reasons which have led your Government to suggest this modification of its original proposal, but I earnestly hope that it is of no particular significance and that it is not to be taken as an indication that the Government of France will find itself unable to join with the Government of the United States in proposing, as suggested above, that the original formula submitted by M. Briand, which envisaged the unqualified renunciation of all war as an instrument of national policy, be made the subject of preliminary discussions with the other great Powers for the purpose of reaching a tentative agreement as to the language to be used in the proposed treaty.

If your Government is agreeable to the plan outlined above and is willing that further discussions of the terms of the proposed multi-lateral treaty be based upon the original proposal submitted to me by M. Briand last June, I have the honour to suggest that the Government of France join with the Government of the United States in a communication to the British, German, Italian and Japanese Governments transmitting the text of M. Briand's original proposal and copies of the subsequent correspondence between the Governments of France and the United States for their consideration and comment, it being understood, of course, that these preliminary discussions would in no way commit any of the participating Governments pending the conclusion of a definitive treaty.

Accept, etc.,

FRANK B. KELLOGG.

VI

M. CLAUDEL TO MR. KELLOGG, JANUARY 21, 1928[1]

January 21, 1928.

MR. SECRETARY OF STATE,

Your Excellency was pleased to inform me, in your Note of the 11th instant, of the consideration suggested to you by my letter of January 5th in answer to your communication of December 28, 1927. My Government has asked me to express to you its satisfaction at the harmonizing, thanks to your Excellency, of the views of the two Governments concerning the best method of accomplishing a project upon the essential principles of which they apparently are in agreement.

The original French proposal of June 1927, contemplating an act confined to France and the United States, appeared to the French Government to be both desirable and feasible by reason of the historical relations between the two Republics.

The American Government was only willing, however, to embody the declaration proposed by the French Government in the preamble of the Franco-American Arbitration Convention now in process of renewal, and considered, on the other hand, for reasons of its own which the French Government has not failed to take into account, that it would be opportune to broaden this manifestation against war, and to make it the subject of a separate act in which the other Powers would be invited to participate.

The Government of the Republic was not opposed to this expansion of its original plan, but it could not but realize, and it felt bound to point out, that the new negotiation as proposed would be more complex and likely to meet with various difficulties.

The question as to whether there would be any advantage in having such an instrument, of a multipartite nature, signed, in the first place, by France and the United States, or else first elaborated by certain of the principal Powers of the world,

[1] From British White Paper, Cmd. 3109, p. 9.

and then presented to all for their signature, is essentially one of procedure.

The Government of the Republic offered a suggestion upon this point because of its desire more speedily and more surely to achieve the result which it seeks in common with the United States. This is tantamount to saying that it is ready to concur in any method which may appear to be the most practicable.

There is, however, a situation of fact to which my Government has requested me to draw your particular attention.

The American Government cannot be unaware of the fact that the great majority of the Powers of the world, and among them most of the principal Powers, are making the organization and strengthening of peace the object of common efforts carried on within the framework of the League of Nations. They are already bound to one another by a Covenant placing them under reciprocal obligations, as well as by agreements such as those signed at Locarno in October 1925, or by international conventions relative to guarantees of neutrality, all of which engagements impose upon them duties which they cannot contravene.

The French proposal of June last, looking to the conclusion of a bi-lateral compact, had been drawn up in the light of the century-old relations between France and the United States; the French Government still stands ready to negotiate with the American Government on the same conditions and on the same basis. It has never altered its attitude in that respect. But when confronted by the initiative of the United States in proposing a multipartite covenant, it had to take into consideration the relations existing among the various Powers which would be called upon to participate therein. This it has done, with the object of assuring the success of the treaty contemplated by the United States. Its suggestions of January 5th as to the terms of the multipartite treaty are inspired by the formula which has already gained the unanimous adherence of all of the States members of the League of Nations, and which for that very reason might be accepted by them with regard to the United States, just as it has already been accepted among themselves.

This is the explanation of our proposal of January 5th.

The Government of the Republic has always, under all circumstances, very clearly and without mental reservation declared its readiness to join in any declaration tending to denounce war as a crime and to set up international sanctions susceptible of preventing or repressing it. There has been no change in its sentiments in that respect; its position remains the same. Your Excellency may, therefore, be assured of its sincere desire to respond to the idea of the American Government, and to second its efforts to the full extent compatible with the situation of fact created by its international obligations. It is this preoccupation which inspired the formula proposed on January 5th, a formula which does, indeed, seem to be the most apt at this time to assure the accomplishment of the American project. The Government of the Republic accordingly cannot but hope that the American Government will share this view. Subject to these observations, the Government of the Republic would, moreover, very gladly welcome any suggestions offered by the American Government which would make it possible to reconcile an absolute condemnation of war with the engagements and obligations assumed by the several nations and the legitimate concern for their respective security.

Pray accept, etc.,

PAUL CLAUDEL.

VII

MR. KELLOGG TO M. CLAUDEL, FEBRUARY 27, 1928[1]

February 27, 1928.

EXCELLENCY,

Our recent discussions of the question whether the United States and France could join in suggesting to the other principal Powers of the world the conclusion of a treaty proscribing war as an instrument of national policy in their mutual relations have been brought by your Note of January 21, 1928, to a point where it seems necessary, if success is to be achieved, to examine the problem from a practical point of view.

It is evident from our previous correspondence that the Governments of France and the United States are of one mind in their earnest desire to initiate and promote a new international movement for effective world peace, and that they are in agreement as to the essential principles of the procedure to be followed in the accomplishment of their common purpose. As I understand your Note of January 21, 1928, the only substantial obstacle in the way of the unqualified acceptance by France of the proposals which I submitted in my Notes of December 28, 1927, and January 11, 1928, is your Government's doubt whether, as a member of the League of Nations and a party to the treaties of Locarno and other treaties guaranteeing neutrality, France can agree with the United States and the other principal world Powers not to resort to war in their mutual relations, without *ipso facto* violating her present international obligations under those treaties. In Your Excellency's last Note this question was suggested for consideration.

Without, of course, undertaking formally to construe the present treaty obligations of France, I desire to point out that, if those obligations can be interpreted so as to permit France to conclude a treaty with the United States such as that offered to me last June by M. Briand and offered again in your Note of January 21, 1928, it is not unreasonable to suppose that they can be interpreted with equal justice so as to permit

[1] From British White Paper, Cmd. 3109, p. 11.

France to join with the United States in offering to conclude an equivalent multi-lateral treaty with the other principal Powers of the world. The difference between the bi-lateral and multi-lateral form of treaty, having for its object the unqualified renunciation of war as an instrument of national policy, seems to me to be one of degree and not of substance. A Government free to conclude such a bi-lateral treaty should be no less able to become a party to an identical multi-lateral treaty, since it is hardly to be presumed that members of the League of Nations are in a position to do separately something they cannot do together. I earnestly hope, therefore, that your Government, which admittedly perceives no bar to the conclusion of an unqualified anti-war treaty with the United States alone, will be able to satisfy itself that an equivalent treaty among the principal world Powers would be equally consistent with membership in the League of Nations. If, however, members of the League of Nations cannot, without violating the terms of the Covenant of the League, agree among themselves and with the Government of the United States to renounce war as an instrument of their national policy, it seems idle to discuss either bi-lateral or multi-lateral treaties unreservedly renouncing war. I am reluctant to believe, however, that the provisions of the Covenant of the League of Nations really stand in the way of the co-operation of the United States and members of the League of Nations in a common effort to abolish the institution of war. Of no little interest in this connexion is the recent adoption of a resolution by the Sixth International Conference of American States expressing, in the name of the American Republics, unqualified condemnation of war as an instrument of national policy in their mutual relations. It is significant to note that, of the twenty-one States represented at the Conference, seventeen are members of the League of Nations.

I trust, therefore, that neither France nor any other member of the League of Nations will finally decide that an unequivocal and unqualified renunciation of war as an instrument of national policy either violates the specific obligations imposed by the

Covenant or conflicts with the fundamental idea and purpose of the League of Nations. On the contrary, is it not entirely reasonable to conclude that a formal engagement of this character, entered into by all of the principal Powers, and ultimately, I trust, by the entire family of nations, would be a most effective instrument for promoting the great ideal of peace which the League itself has so closely at heart? If, however, such a declaration were accompanied by definitions of the word "aggressor," and by exceptions and qualifications stipulating when nations would be justified in going to war, its effect would be very greatly weakened, and its positive value as a guarantee of peace virtually destroyed. The ideal which inspires the effort so sincerely and so hopefully put forward by your Government and mine is arresting and appealing just because of its purity and simplicity, and I cannot avoid the feeling that, if Governments should publicly acknowledge that they can only deal with this ideal in a technical spirit and must insist upon the adoption of reservations impairing, if not utterly destroying, the true significance of their common endeavours, they would be in effect only recording their impotence, to the keen disappointment of mankind in general.

From the broad standpoint of humanity and civilization all war is an assault upon the stability of human society and should be suppressed in the common interest. The Government of the United States desires to see the institution of war abolished, and stands ready to conclude with the French, British, Italian, German, and Japanese Governments a single multi-lateral treaty, open to subsequent adherence by any and all other Governments, binding the parties thereto not to resort to war with one another. The precise language to be employed in such a treaty is a matter of indifference to the United States, so long as it clearly and unmistakably sets forth the determination of the parties to abolish war among themselves. I therefore renew the suggestion contained in my Note of January 11, 1928, that the Government of France join with the Government of the United States in transmitting to the British, Italian, German, and Japanese Governments, for their consideration and comment, the text of M. Briand's original proposal, together with copies of the subsequent correspondence between France and the United States, as a basis for preliminary discussions looking to the conclusion of an appropriate multilateral treaty proscribing recourse to war.

Accept, etc.,
FRANK B. KELLOGG.

VIII

EXTRACT FROM AN ADDRESS GIVEN BY MR. KELLOGG
  BEFORE THE COUNCIL ON FOREIGN RELATIONS, NEW
  YORK, MARCH 15, 1928[1]

. . . As you are all aware, in a communication dated June 20, 1927, M. Briand proposed to the United States the conclusion of a bi-lateral treaty under the terms of which France and the United States would agree to renounce war as an instrument of their national policy towards each other. The treaty read as follows :—

> The high contracting Powers solemnly declare, in the name of the French people and the people of the United States of America, that they condemn recourse to war and renounce it respectively as an instrument of their national policy towards each other.
> The settlement or the solution of all disputes or conflicts, of whatever nature or of whatever origin they may be, which may arise between France and the United States of America, shall never be sought by either side except by pacific means.

This important and inspiring proposal was carefully and sympathetically studied by the Government of the United States. While we might well have hesitated to take the initiative in proposing such a treaty to Europe, the invitation from France afforded us an opportunity to examine anew the whole question of world peace and to determine in what practical manner we could best co-operate. We made that examination, and in my Note of December 28, 1927, after expressing the sincere appreciation of the United States for the offer which France had so impressively submitted, I warmly seconded M. Briand's proposition that war be formally renounced as an instrument of national policy, but suggested that instead of giving effect thereto in a bi-lateral treaty between France and the United States, an equivalent multi-lateral treaty be concluded among the principal Powers of the world, open to adherence by any and all nations, thus extending throughout the world the benefits of a covenant originally suggested as between France and the United States alone. The Powers

[1] From Special Supplement to *Foreign Affairs*, vol. vi, No. 3, pp. vii–xi.

which I suggested be invited in the first instance to join with France and the United States in such a treaty were Great Britain, Germany, Italy, and Japan.

France, I am happy to say, promptly agreed in principle to the idea of a multi-lateral treaty. France suggested, however, that the treaty provide only for the renunciation of wars of aggression, explaining that while France could conclude a bi-lateral treaty with the United States providing for the unqualified renunciation of war, the conclusion of a similar multi-lateral treaty presented certain difficulties in view of the obligations of France under the Covenant of the League of Nations, treaties such as those signed at Locarno in October 1925, and other international conventions relating to guarantees of neutrality. The French Government also pointed out that in September 1927 the members of the League of Nations adopted a resolution condemning aggressive war as an international crime. In these circumstances France expressed the opinion that the common object of the two Governments could best be attained by framing the proposed anti-war treaty so as to cover wars of aggression only. I have not been able to agree to that reservation.

My objection to limiting the scope of an anti-war treaty to mere wars of aggression is based partly upon a very real disinclination to see the ideal of world peace qualified in any way, and partly upon the absence of any satisfactory definition of the word "aggressor" or the phrase "wars of aggression." It is difficult for me to see how a definition could be agreed upon which would not be open to abuse. The danger inherent in every definition is recognized by the British Government, which in a memorandum recently submitted to the Sub-committee on Security of the Preparatory Commission on Disarmament of the League of Nations discussed attempted definitions of this character, and quoted from a speech by the British Foreign Secretary in which Sir Austen said: "I therefore remain opposed to this attempt to define the aggressor because I believe that it will be a trap for the innocent and a signpost for the guilty." I agree with Sir Austen on this point.

It seems to me that any attempt to define the word "aggres‿ sor" and by exceptions and qualifications to stipulate when nations are justified in going to war with one another, would greatly weaken the effect of any treaty such as that under consideration and virtually destroy its positive value as a guarantee of peace. And in my last Note to the French Government I stated expressly that I could not avoid the feeling that if Governments should publicly acknowledge that they could only deal with this ideal of world peace in a technical spirit and must insist upon the adoption of reservations impairing if not utterly destroying the true significance of their common endeavours, they would be in effect only recording their impotence, to the keen disappointment of mankind in general.

In my Note of February 27, 1928, I also discussed at some length the question raised by the Government of France whether, as a member of the League of Nations and as a party to the treaties of Locarno and other treaties guaranteeing neutrality, France could agree with the United States and the other principal world Powers not to resort to war in their mutual relations without *ipso facto* violating their present obligations under those treaties. I pointed out that if those treaty obligations could be interpreted so as to permit France to conclude with the United States alone a treaty such as that proposed by M. Briand, it was not unreasonable to suppose that they could be interpreted with equal justice so as to permit France to join with the United States in offering to conclude an equivalent multi-lateral treaty with the other principal Powers of the world. I stated that it seemed to me that the difference between the bi-lateral and multi-lateral form of treaty, having for its object the unqualified renunciation of war, was one of degree and not of substance, and that a Government able to conclude such a bi-lateral treaty would be no less able to become a party to an identical multi-lateral treaty, since it could hardly be presumed that members of the League of Nations were in a position to do separately something that they could not do together.

In these circumstances I expressed the earnest hope that France, which admittedly perceives no bar to the conclusion of an unqualified anti-war treaty with the United States alone, would be able to satisfy itself that an equivalent treaty among the principal world Powers would be equally consistent with membership in the League of Nations, adding that if members of the League of Nations could not, without violating the terms of the Covenant, agree among themselves and with the United States to renounce war as an instrument of their national policy, it seemed idle to discuss either bi-lateral or multi-lateral treaties unreservedly renouncing war. In that connection I call attention to the fact that twenty-one American States represented at the recent Havana Conference adopted a resolution unqualifiedly condemning war as an instrument of national policy in their mutual relations, and to the fact that seventeen of the twenty-one States represented at that Conference are members of the League of Nations.

I concluded my Note with the unequivocal statement that the Government of the United States desires to see the institution of war abolished and stands ready to conclude with the French, British, Italian, German, and Japanese Governments a single multi-lateral treaty open to subsequent adhesion by any and all other Governments binding the parties thereto not to resort to war with one another. This is the position of the Government of the United States, and this is the object which we are seeking to attain.

I cannot believe that such a treaty would violate the terms of the League Covenant or conflict with the obligations of the members of the League. Even Article 10 of the Covenant has been construed to mean that League members are not inescapably bound thereby to employ their military forces. According to a recent statement by the British Government, many members of the League accept as a proper interpretation of Article 10 a resolution submitted to the Fourth Assembly but not formally adopted owing to one adverse vote. That resolution stated explicitly:—

"It is for the constitutional authorities of each member to decide, in reference to the obligation of preserving the independence and the integrity of the territory of members, in what degree the member is bound to assure the execution of this obligation by employment of its military forces."

I earnestly hope, therefore, that the present negotiations, looking to the conclusion of an unqualified multi-lateral anti-war treaty, may ultimately achieve success, and I have no doubt that if the principal Powers of the world are united in a sincere desire to consummate such a treaty, a formula can be devised which will be acceptable to them all. Since, however, the purpose of the United States is so far as possible to eliminate war as a factor in international relations, I cannot state too emphatically that it will not become a party to any agreement which directly or indirectly, expressly or by implication, is a military alliance. The United States cannot obligate itself in advance to use its armed forces against any other nation of the world. It does not believe that the peace of the world or of Europe depends upon or can be assured by treaties of military alliance. The futility of such as guarantors of peace is repeatedly demonstrated in the pages of history.

I must not claim that treaties of arbitration and of conciliation, or even treaties explicitly renouncing war as an instrument of national policy, afford a certain guarantee against those conflicts between nations which have periodically broken out since the dawn of world history. In addition to treaties there must be an aroused public conscience against the utter horror and frightfulness of war. The peoples of the world must enjoy a peaceful mind, as it has been said, and treaties such as those I have discussed this evening, and the efforts of statesmen to advance the cause of world peace, can only be regarded as a portion of the problem. I am not so blind as to believe that the millennium has arrived, but I do believe that the world is making great strides towards the pacific adjustment of international disputes and that the common people are of one mind in their desire to see the abolition of war as an institution. Certainly the United States should not be backward in promoting this new movement for world peace, and both personally and officially, as Secretary of State, I shall always support and advocate the conclusion of appropriate treaties for arbitration, for conciliation, and for the renunciation of war.

IX

M. CLAUDEL TO MR. KELLOGG, MARCH 26, 1928[1]

MR. SECRETARY OF STATE,

In reply to your Note of February 27th last, regarding the proposal for a multi-lateral treaty proscribing war, I have the honour to inform Your Excellency that M. Briand has been pleased to find in the observations which you have submitted for his consideration a new and cordial affirmation of the common inspiration which animates our two Governments, equally anxious to co-operate in an international movement toward the effective establishment of peace in the world. Assured of such solidarity in the pursuit of an identical purpose, M. Briand remains convinced, as does Your Excellency, that a mutually acceptable formula may well result from the exchange of views which has taken place up to now between our two Governments, if on both sides there is a disposition to adhere to those essential realities which must be preserved in this discussion, by subordinating thereto those differences of form to which questions of terminology not affecting the substance of the discussion may upon analysis be reduced.

That is to say, that the French Government at this point of the discussion, when all the aspects of the problem have been examined, proposes to adopt as practical a point of view as possible and to facilitate as far as it can the effort of the American Government in the direction of an immediate decision.

The observations which M. Briand has ventured to offer in support of his last suggestion were inspired by a very sincere desire to facilitate in a practical manner the realization of the proposal for the contemplated multi-lateral treaty by pointing out the conditions best adapted to bring about the consent thereto of all the Governments whose agreement is necessary. The French wording, therefore, tending to limit to war of aggression the proscription proposed in the form of a multi-lateral rather than a bi-lateral treaty, was intended to obviate in so far as the American plan was concerned those serious

[1] From British White Paper, Cmd. 3109, p. 17.

difficulties which would assuredly be encountered in practice. In order to pay due regard to the international obligations of the signatories, it was not possible, as soon as it became a question of a multi-lateral treaty, to impart thereto the unconditional character desired by Your Excellency without facing the necessity of obtaining the unanimous adherence of all the existing States, or at least of all the interested States, that is to say, those which by reason of their situation are exposed to the possibility of a conflict with any one of the contracting States. In the relations between the States of the American continent there are similar difficulties which led the American Government at the Pan-American Conference at Habana to approve a resolution limited to the very terms "war of aggression" which the French Government felt compelled to use in characterizing the renunciation to which it was requested to bind itself by means of a multi-lateral treaty. To be sure, the same reservation does not appear in another resolution to which Your Excellency referred in your Note of February 27th, but it must be observed that this resolution in itself constituted only a kind of preliminary tending toward a treaty of arbitration with regard to which numerous reservations were formulated.

Your Excellency appears to have been surprised that France should not be able to conclude with all the Powers in the form of a multi-lateral treaty the same treaty which she offered to conclude separately with the United States in the form of a bilateral treaty. My Government believes that it has explained this point with sufficient clearness in recalling the fact that the project of a treaty of perpetual friendship between France and the United States proposed last June was drafted in such a way as to limit strictly the mutual undertakings which it contained to those relations in law resulting from intercourse between the two signatory States alone. Within such limits an absolutely unconditional agreement might be entered into, since that agreement would not expose the signatories, as would a multi-lateral treaty, to juridical difficulties resulting from the respective positions of various Powers with regard to one another, and since, furthermore, as regards two countries like France and the United States, morally united as they are by ties of time-honoured friendship, other contractual engagements concluded by one or the other Power could never constitute in fact anything but purely theoretical obstacles.

In order to attain the result which Your Excellency has in view, you have considered it preferable to adhere to the conception of a multi-lateral treaty, and you have deemed it necessary to insist that even in the multi-lateral form the proposed treaty should include an unconditional pledge. If Your Excellency really believes that greater chances of success may be found in this formula in spite of the consequences which it involves, especially the necessity of attaining a treaty world-wide in its scope, the French Government would hesitate to discuss longer the question of its adherence to a plan which the American Government originated and for which it is responsible. Without in any way losing sight of its international obligations, both as a member of the League of Nations and as a party to the treaties of Locarno or treaties guaranteeing neutrality, France, for the purpose of finding a common basis for initial negotiations, is wholly disposed, after a new examination of the proposals formulated by Your Excellency, to suggest immediately to the German, British, Italian, and Japanese Governments that they join in seeking, in the spirit and in the letter of the last American Note, any adjustments which in the last analysis may be forthcoming with respect to the possibility of reconciling previous obligations with the terms of the contemplated new treaty.

The French Government notes at once with satisfaction that while advocating the conclusion among the Governments specifically mentioned of a treaty binding the signatories not to resort to war, the Government of the United States admits the participation in that treaty of all the other Governments of the world. This conception accords with a reservation actually necessary for obtaining a real instrument for the establishment of peace by means of a formal engagement among all Powers among whom political controversies may arise. Such an engagement would in fact involve the risk of exposing the signatories to dangers and misunderstandings unless based upon the complete equality in the application of the treaty among themselves of all the States with respect to other States and not only upon the equality of certain States among them. The treaty contemplated could not operate in respect of one Power which is a party thereto unless the other States exposed to the possibility of grave controversies with that party were also signatories thereof.

At the same time it is clear that in order not to turn an instrument of progress and peace into a means of oppression, if one of the signatory States should fail to keep its word, the other signatories should be released from their engagement with respect to the offending State. On this second point, as on the first, the French Government believes itself fully in accord with the Government of the United States.

My Government likewise gathers from the declarations which Your Excellency was good enough to make to me on March 1st last, the assurance that the renunciation of war, thus proclaimed, would not deprive the signatories of the right of legitimate defence. Such an interpretation tends to dissipate apprehensions, and the French Government is happy to note it.

If such is the attitude of the American Government on these three fundamental points, and if it is clearly understood in a general way that the obligations of the new pact should not be substituted for, or prejudice in any way, previous obligations contained in international instruments such as the Covenant of the League of Nations, the Locarno agreements or treaties guaranteeing neutrality whose character and scope cannot be modified thereby, then the differences of opinion which have appeared in the course of previous phases of the negotiation have to do more with words than with the reality of the problem facing the two Governments to-day.

Hence, in accordance with the proposal contained in your Note of January 11th, which you kindly renewed in your Note of February 27th, the French Government would be prepared forthwith to ioin with the Government of the United

States in submitting for the consideration of the Governments of Germany, Great Britain, Italy, and Japan the correspondence exchanged between France and the United States since June 1927, and in proposing at the same time, for the assent of the four Governments, a draft agreement essentially corresponding in purpose to the original proposal of M. Briand, in the multipartite form desired by the United States with the changes of wording made necessary by the new concept; the signatory Powers of such an instrument, while not prejudicing their rights of legitimate defence within the framework of existing treaties, should make a solemn declaration condemning recourse to war as an instrument of national policy, or in other words as a means of carrying out their own spontaneous, independent policy.

They would specifically undertake, among themselves, to refrain from any attack or invasion, and never to seek the settlement of any difference or conflict of whatsoever nature or origin which might arise between them save by pacific means. It would, however, be clearly understood that an obligation could only exist for the signatories in the event that the engagement were contracted by all States, that is to say, that the treaty, open to the accession of all Powers, would only come into force after having received universal acceptance, unless the Powers having signed this treaty or acceded thereto should agree upon its coming into force, despite certain abstentions. Finally, in case one of the contracting Powers should happen to contravene the treaty, the other contracting Powers would be automatically relieved, with respect to that Power, of the obligations contained in the treaty.

It is in this form, it would seem, that the negotiations of a plan for a multi-lateral pact such as conceived by the American Government could be pursued with the greatest chances of success. Your Excellency may be assured, in any case, in the conduct of this negotiation of the most sincere and most complete collaboration of my Government, which is always ready to associate itself, without ambiguity or reservation, with any solemn and formal undertaking tending to ensure, strengthen, or extend the effective solidarity of the nations in the cause of peace.

In responding to these ideas, whose happy inspiration cannot be gainsaid, France would feel confident that she was continuing the work to which she has never ceased to apply herself in her foreign policy, and, faithful to her previous international engagements of that nature, that she was contributing nobly, as Your Excellency has said, in "promoting the great ideal of peace which the League itself has so closely at heart."

Pray accept, etc.,

CLAUDEL.

X

MR. HOUGHTON, AMERICAN AMBASSADOR IN LONDON, TO SIR AUSTEN CHAMBERLAIN[1]

UNITED STATES EMBASSY, LONDON,
April 13, 1928.

SIR,

As you are aware, there has recently been exchanged between the Governments of France and the United States a series of Notes dealing with the question of a possible international renunciation of war. The views of the two Governments have been clearly set forth in the correspondence between the two.

The Government of the United States, as stated in its Note of February 27, 1928, desires to see the institution of war abolished and stands ready to conclude with the French, British, German, Italian, and Japanese Governments a single multi-lateral treaty, open to subsequent adherence by any and all other Governments, binding the parties thereto not to resort to war with one another.

The Government of the French Republic, while no less eager to promote the cause of world peace and to co-operate with other nations in any practical movement towards that end, has pointed out certain considerations which, in its opinion, must be borne in mind by those Powers which are members of the League of Nations, parties to the treaties of Locarno, parties to other treaties guaranteeing neutrality. My Government has not conceded that such considerations necessitate any modifications of its proposal for a multi-lateral treaty, and is of the opinion that every nation in the world can, with a proper regard for its own interests as well as for the interests of the entire family of nations, join in such a treaty. It believes, moreover, that the execution by France, Great Britain, Germany, Italy, Japan, and the United States of a treaty solemnly renouncing war in favour of the pacific settlement of international controversies would have tremendous moral effect

[1] From British White Paper, Cmd. 3109, p. 2.

and ultimately lead to the adherence of all the other countries of the world.

The discussions which have taken place between France and the United States have thus reached a point where it seems essential, if ultimate success is to be attained, that the British, German, Italian, and Japanese Governments should each have an opportunity formally to decide to what extent, if any, its existing commitments constitute a bar to its participation with the United States in an unqualified renunciation of war. In these circumstances, the Government of the United States, having reached complete agreement with the Government of the French Republic as to this procedure, has instructed me formally to transmit herewith for the consideration of His Majesty's Government the text of M. Briand's original proposal of last June, together with copies of the Notes subsequently exchanged between France and the United States on the subject of a multi-lateral treaty for the renunciation of war. I have also been instructed by my Government to transmit herewith for consideration a preliminary draft of a treaty representing in a general way the form of treaty which the Government of the United States is prepared to sign with the French, British, German, Italian, and Japanese Governments and any other Government similarly disposed. It will be observed that the language of Articles I and II of this draft treaty is practically identical with that of the corresponding articles in the treaty which M. Briand proposed to the United States.

The Government of the United States would be pleased to be informed as promptly as may be convenient whether His Majesty's Government is in a position to give favourable consideration to the conclusion of a treaty such as that transmitted herewith, and if not, what specific modifications in the text thereof would make it acceptable.

I have, etc.,

A. B. HOUGHTON.

XI

A COMPARISON OF THE AMERICAN AND FRENCH [1] DRAFT TREATIES FOR THE OUTLAWRY OF WAR

AMERICAN DRAFT.

The President of the United States of America, the President of the French Republic, H.M. the King of Great Britain, Ireland and the British Dominions beyond the Seas, Emperor of India, the President of the German Empire, H.M. the King of Italy, H.M. the Emperor of Japan,

Deeply sensible that their high office imposes upon them a solemn duty to promote the welfare of mankind;

Inspired by a common desire not only to perpetuate the peaceful and friendly relations now happily subsisting between their peoples, but also to prevent war among any of the nations of the world;

Desirous by formal act to bear unmistakable witness that they condemn war as an instrument of national policy and renounce it in favour of the pacific settlement of international disputes;

Hopeful that, encouraged by their example, all the other nations of the world will join in this humane endeavour and, by adhering to the present treaty as soon as it comes into force, bring their peoples within the scope of its beneficent provisions, thus uniting the civilized nations of the world in a common renunciation of war as an instrument of their national policy;

Have decided to conclude a treaty, and, for that purpose, have

FRENCH DRAFT.

The President of the United States of America, the President of the French Republic, H.M. the King of Great Britain, Ireland and the British Dominions, Emperor of India, the President of the German Empire, H.M. the King of Italy, H.M. the Emperor of Japan,

Inspired by a common desire not only to perpetuate the peaceful and friendly relations now happily subsisting between their peoples, but also to remove the danger of war among all the nations of the world;

Having agreed to affirm, in a solemn declaration, their most formal and clear resolve to condemn war as an instrument of national policy and so renounce it in favour of the peaceful settlement of international disputes and formulating the hope that all the other nations of the world will be ready to take part in this humane effort to achieve the union of the civilized peoples in a single renunciation of war as an instrument of national policy,

have decided to conclude a Treaty, and to this end have respectively

[1] From *Bulletin of International News*, vol. iv, No. 23, pp. 10–12, May 12, 1928.

AMERICAN DRAFT—*continued.*

appointed as their respective plenipotentiaries the President of the United States of America, etc., . . .

Who, having communicated to one another their full powers, found in good and due form, have agreed upon the following articles:

Article I.

The High Contracting Parties

solemnly declare, in the name of their respective peoples, that they condemn the recourse to war for the solution of international controversies and renounce it as an instrument of national policy in their relations with one another.

Article II.

The High Contracting Parties agree that the settlement or solution of all disputes or conflicts, of whatever nature or of whatever origin they may be, which may arise among them, shall never be sought except by pacific means.

FRENCH DRAFT—*continued.*

chosen as their plenipotentiary representatives—

Who, having exchanged their credentials in due form, have agreed to the following articles:

Article I.

The High Contracting Parties, without prejudice to their right of legitimate defence within the scope of existing treaties, especially when these define the violation of certain of their articles as a hostile act, solemnly declare that they condemn recourse to war and renounce it as an instrument of national policy, that is to say, as the instrument of any personal, spontaneous, and independent political action which they may initiate and not as that of an action into which they may be drawn by the application of a Treaty registered by the League of Nations. They undertake in these terms not to indulge in any attack or invasion against one another.

Article II.

The settlement or solution of disputes or conflicts of any nature or origin whatever which may arise between the High Contracting Parties or between any two of them shall never be sought on either side except by peaceful means.

Article III.

In case one of the High Contracting Parties should violate the present Treaty, the other contracting Powers shall be completely set free, as regards that Party, from the engagements of this Treaty.

Article IV.

The provisions of the present Treaty shall not modify any of the rights and obligations imposed upon the Contracting Powers by the international agreements to which they are parties.

Article V.

The present Treaty shall be offered to all the Powers for their signature, and shall have no binding force until it has been generally accepted, unless the present signatory Powers, in agreement with those which join them hereafter, agree to put the Treaty into force in spite of certain abstentions.

Article III.

The present Treaty shall be ratified by the High Contracting Parties named in the Preamble in accordance with their respective constitutional requirements and shall take effect as between them as soon as all their several instruments of ratification shall have been deposited at . . .

This Treaty shall, when it has come into effect, as prescribed in the preceding paragraph, remain open as long as may be necessary for adherence by all the other Powers of the world. Every instrument evidencing the adherence of a Power shall be deposited at . . . and the Treaty shall, immediately upon such deposit, become effective as between the Powers thus adhering and the Powers parties hereto.

Article VI.

The present Treaty shall be ratified. Ratifications shall be deposited at . . . within three months from the date of ratification. It will be brought by the . . . Government to the notice of all the Powers with an invitation to accept it. The . . . Government will deliver to each of the signatory Powers and to the Powers which have associated themselves with the Treaty a certified copy of the Treaty.

One year after the expiry of the period referred to in Article V, the . . . Government will address a complete list of signatures and acceptances to all the Powers which have signed or accepted the Treaty.

AMERICAN DRAFT—*continued.*

It shall be the duty of the Government of . . . to furnish each Government named in the Preamble and every Government subsequently adhering to this Treaty, with a certified copy of the Treaty and of every instrument of ratification or adherence. It shall also be the duty of the Government of . . . telegraphically to notify such Governments immediately upon the deposit with it of each instrument of ratification or adherence.

In faith whereof the respective plenipotentiaries have signed this Treaty in the French and English languages, both texts having equal force, and hereunto affixed their seals.

Done at . . . the . . . day of . . . in the Year of Our Lord One thousand nine hundred and twenty- . . .

SPEECH MADE BY MR. KELLOGG BEFORE THE AMERICAN INTERNATIONAL LAW ASSOCIATION, WASHINGTON, APRIL 29, 1928[1]

There seem to be six major considerations which the French Government has emphasized in its correspondence and in its draft treaty, namely, that the treaty must not (1) impair the right of legitimate self-defence; (2) violate the Covenant of the League of Nations; (3) violate the treaties of Locarno; (4) violate certain unspecified treaties guaranteeing neutrality; (5) bind the parties in respect of a State breaking the Treaty; (6) come into effect until accepted by all, or substantially all, of the Powers of the world. The views of the United States on these six points are as follows:—

(1) *Self-Defence.*—There is nothing in the American draft of an anti-war treaty which restricts or impairs in any way the right of self-defence. That right is inherent in every sovereign State and is implicit in every treaty. Every nation is free at all times and regardless of treaty provisions to defend its territory from attack or invasion, and it alone is competent to decide whether circumstances require recourse to war in self-defence.

If it has a good case the world will applaud and not condemn its action. Express recognition by treaty of this inalienable right, however, gives rise to the same difficulty encountered in any effort to define aggression. It is the identical question approached from the other side. Inasmuch as no treaty provision can add to the natural right of self-defence, it is not in the interest of peace that a treaty should stipulate a juristic conception of self-defence, since it is far too easy for the unscrupulous to mould events to accord with an agreed definition.

(2) *The League Covenant.*—The Covenant imposes no affirmative primary obligation to go to war. The obligation, if any, is secondary and attaches only when deliberately accepted by a State. Article X of the Covenant has, for example, been interpreted by a resolution submitted to the fourth Assembly,

[1] From *New York Herald and Tribune,* April 30, 1928.

but not formally adopted owing to one adverse vote, to mean that "it is for the constitutional authorities of each member to decide in reference to the obligation of preserving the independence and the integrity of the territory of members, in what degree the member is bound to assure the execution of this obligation by employment of its military forces."

There is, in my opinion, no necessary inconsistency between the Covenant and the idea of an unqualified renunciation of war. The Covenant can, it is true, be construed as authorizing war in certain circumstances, but it is an authorization and not a positive requirement.

(3) *The Treaties of Locarno.*—If the parties to the treaties of Locarno are under any positive obligation to go to war, such obligation certainly would not attach until one of the parties has resorted to war in violation of its solemn pledges thereunder. It is therefore obvious that if all the parties to the Locarno treaties become parties to the multi-lateral anti-war treaty proposed by the United States there would be a double assurance that the Locarno treaties would not be violated by recourse to arms.

In such event it would follow that resort to war by any State in violation of the Locarno treaties would also be a breach of the multi-lateral anti-war treaty, and the other parties to the anti-war treaty would thus, as a matter of law, be automatically released from their obligations thereunder and free to fulfil their Locarno commitments.

The United States is entirely willing that all parties to the Locarno treaties should become parties to its proposed anti-war treaty, either through signature, in the first instance, or by immediate accession to the treaty as soon as it comes into force in the manner provided in Article III of the American draft, and it will offer no objection when and if such suggestion is made.

(4) *Treaties of Neutrality.*—The United States is not informed as to the precise treaties which France has in mind, and cannot therefore discuss their provisions. It is not unreasonable to suppose, however, that the relations between France

and the States whose neutrality she has guaranteed are sufficiently close and intimate to make it possible for France to persuade such States to adhere seasonably to the anti-war treaty proposed by the United States. If this were done, no party to the anti-war treaty could attack the neutralized States without violating the treaty and thereby automatically freeing France and the other Powers in respect of the treaty-breaking State from the obligations of the anti-war treaty.

If the neutralized States were attacked by a State not a party to the anti-war treaty, France would be as free to act under the treaties guaranteeing neutrality as if she were not a party to the anti-war treaty. It is difficult to perceive, therefore, how treaties guaranteeing neutrality can be regarded as necessarily preventing the conclusion by France or any other Power of a multi-lateral treaty for the renunciation of war.

(5) *Relations with a Treaty-breaking State.*—As I have already pointed out, there can be no question as a matter of law that violation of a multi-lateral anti-war treaty through resort to war by one party thereto would automatically release the other parties from their obligations to the treaty-breaking State. Any express recognition of this principle of law is wholly unnecessary.

(6) *Universality.*—From the beginning it has been the hope of the United States that its proposed multi-lateral anti-war treaty should be world-wide in its application, and appropriate provision therefor was made in the draft submitted to the other Governments on April 13th. From a practical standpoint it is clearly preferable, however, not to postpone the coming into force of an anti-war treaty until all the nations of the world can agree upon the text of such a treaty and cause it to be ratified. For one reason or another a State so situated as to be no menace to the peace of the world might obstruct agreement or delay ratification in such manner as to render abortive the efforts of all the other Powers.

It is highly improbable, moreover, that a form of treaty acceptable to the British, French, German, Italian, and Japanese Governments, as well as to the United States, would not be equally acceptable to most, if not all, of the other Powers of the world.

Even were this not the case, however, the coming into force among the above-named six Powers of an effective anti-war treaty and their observance thereof would be a practical guarantee against a second world war. This in itself would be a tremendous service to humanity, and the United States is not willing to jeopardize the practical success of the proposal which it has made by conditioning the coming into force of the treaty upon prior universal or almost universal acceptance.

XIII

REPLY OF THE GERMAN GOVERNMENT, APRIL 27, 1928[1]

April 27, 1928.[1]

YOUR EXCELLENCY,

In your Note of April 15th and its annexes you informed me of the negotiations between the Government of the United States of America and the French Government for the conclusion of an international pact for the outlawry of war. At the same time you put me the question whether the German Government were disposed to conclude such a pact in accordance with the draft drawn up by the United States Government, or whether it considered certain alterations in this draft necessary.

The German Government has examined your request with the care demanded by the extraordinary importance of the occasion. In the course of this examination it was able to take into account the draft treaty that in the meantime had been drawn up by the French Government and transmitted to the interested Powers. As the result of the examination I beg to make to you the following communication in the name of the German Government:—

The German Government most warmly welcomes the opening of negotiations for the conclusion of an international pact for the outlawry of war. The two great ideas that lie at the basis of the initiative of the French Foreign Minister and the proposal of the United States Government to which it gave rise entirely correspond to the principles of German policy. Germany has no higher interest than the possibility of seeing military conflicts eliminated and such a development ensured in the life of the peoples as guarantees a peaceful settlement of all disputes between States. The conclusion of a pact of the kind that the United States Government now has in view would certainly bring the peoples considerably nearer to the attainment of this aim.

As the need of the peoples to secure peace has since the

---

[1] From *The Times*, May 1, 1928.

end of the World War already led to other international agreements, the necessity arises for the States that have taken part in them to elucidate in what relation the pact now proposed would stand to these international agreements that are already in force.

You have called attention in your Note, Mr. Ambassador, to the considerations expressed by the French Government in its exchange of views with the Government of the United States. So far as Germany is concerned, it is the Covenant of the League of Nations and the Rhine Pact of Locarno that come into consideration as international agreements which have a bearing on the new pact; Germany has undertaken no other international commitments of this kind. Respect for the obligations arising out of the Covenant of the League of Nations and the Rhine Pact must in the view of the German Government stand immutable. The German Government is, however, convinced that these obligations contain nothing that could in any way conflict with the obligations implied in the draft treaty of the United States. On the contrary, it believes that the binding obligation not to use war as an instrument of national policy would only be calculated to strengthen the basic idea of the League Covenant and the Rhine Pact.

The German Government takes it for granted that a pact of the kind proposed by the United States would not place in doubt the sovereign right of each State to defend itself.

It goes without saying that if any State breaks the pact the other contracting parties recover their freedom of action in regard to that State. The State affected by the infringement of the pact is therefore not prevented from taking arms on its part against the peace-breakers. It does not appear to the German Government necessary in a pact of this kind expressly to provide for the case of its infringement.

In agreement with the United States Government and with the French Government, the German Government is also of the opinion that the ultimate aim must be the universality of the new pact. If the States primarily held in view as signatory Powers conclude the pact it may be expected that the other

States will very soon take advantage of the right to adhere that is accorded to them without restriction or condition.

The German Government can accordingly declare that it is ready to conclude a pact as proposed by the United States and to engage with the interested Governments in the negotiations necessary for this purpose. The German Government associates with this declaration the definite expectation that the conclusion of a pact of such scope will not fail to exert an influence very speedily on the shaping of international relations. Thus this new guarantee for the maintenance of peace must give an effective impulse to the endeavours to bring about general disarmament. Furthermore, the abandonment of war must contribute to the development, as a necessary counterpart, of means for settling in a peaceful manner conflicts of national interests that now exist or may arise in the future.

XIV

REPLY OF THE ITALIAN GOVERNMENT[1]

May 5, 1928.

YOUR EXCELLENCY,

I have the honour to refer to my Note of April 23rd, relative to the proposal of the United States Government regarding a multi-lateral anti-war treaty.

I hardly need to assure you that Italy, adhering to the policy which she is constantly following, has welcomed with lively sympathy this initiative and offers very willingly her cordial collaboration towards reaching an agreement.

Your Excellency is aware of the fact that there is under consideration the proposal for a preliminary meeting of the legal experts of the Powers whose direct interest in the proposed treaty has been enlisted. The Royal Government has adhered to this procedure, but has clearly pointed out that in its opinion such a meeting can only be effective if the participation of a legal expert of the Government of the United States is assured.

In accordance with this order of ideas I beg Your Excellency to communicate to Mr. Kellogg the lively desire of the Royal Government that the participation of the United States in the preliminary meeting mentioned above be not lacking.

MUSSOLINI.

[1] From Canadian White Paper, p. 20.

XV

REPLY OF THE BRITISH GOVERNMENT, MAY 19, 1928[1]

Sir Austen Chamberlain to Mr. Houghton

FOREIGN OFFICE,
May 19, 1928.

YOUR EXCELLENCY,

Your Note of April 13th, containing the text of a draft treaty for the renunciation of war, together with copies of the correspondence between the United States and French Governments on the subject of this treaty, has been receiving sympathetic consideration at the hands of His Majesty's Government in Great Britain. A Note has also been received from the French Government, containing certain suggestions for discussion in connection with the proposed treaty, and the German Government were good enough to send me a copy of the reply which has been made by them to the proposals of the United States Government.

2. The suggestion for the conclusion of a treaty for the renunciation of war as an instrument of national policy has evoked widespread interest in this country, and His Majesty's Government will support the movement to the utmost of their power.

3. After making a careful study of the text contained in Your Excellency's Note and of the amended text suggested in the French Note, His Majesty's Government feel convinced that there is no serious divergence between the effect of these two drafts. This impression is confirmed by a study of the text of the speech by the Secretary of State of the United States to which Your Excellency drew my attention, and which he delivered before the American Society of International Law on April 28th. The aim of the United States Government, as I understand it, is to embody in a treaty a broad statement of principle, to proclaim without restriction or qualification that war shall not be used as an instrument of policy. With this aim His Majesty's Government are wholly in accord. The French

---

[1] From British White Paper, Cmd. 3109, p. 23.

proposals, equally imbued with the same purpose, have merely added an indication of certain exceptional circumstances in which the violation of that principle by one party may oblige the others to take action seeming at first sight to be inconsistent with the terms of the proposed pact. His Majesty's Government appreciate the scruples which have prompted these suggestions by the French Government. The exact fulfilment of treaty engagements is a matter which affects the national honour; precision as to the scope of such engagements is, therefore, of importance. Each of the suggestions made by the French Government has been carefully considered from this point of view.

4. After studying the wording of Article 1 of the United States draft, His Majesty's Government do not think that its terms exclude action which a State may be forced to take in self-defence. Mr. Kellogg has made it clear in the speech to which I have referred above that he regards the right of self-defence as inalienable, and His Majesty's Government are disposed to think that on this question no addition to the text is necessary.

5. As regards the text of Article 2, no appreciable difference is found between the American and the French proposals. His Majesty's Government are, therefore, content to accept the former if, as they understand to be the case, a dispute "among the high contracting parties" is a phrase wide enough to cover a dispute between any two of them.

6. The French Note suggests the addition of an Article providing that violation of the treaty by one of the parties should release the remainder from their obligations under the treaty towards that party. His Majesty's Government are not satisfied that, if the treaty stood alone, the addition of some such provision would not be necessary. Mr. Kellogg's speech, however, shows that he put forward for acceptance the text of the proposed treaty upon the understanding that violation of the undertaking by one party would free the remaining parties from the obligation to observe its terms in respect of the treaty-breaking State.

7. If it is agreed that this is the principle which will apply in

the case of this particular treaty, His Majesty's Government are satisfied and will not ask for the insertion of any amendment. Means can no doubt be found without difficulty of placing this understanding on record in some appropriate manner so that it may have equal value with the terms of the treaty itself.

8. The point is one of importance because of its bearing on the treaty engagements by which His Majesty's Government are already bound. The preservation of peace has been the chief concern of His Majesty's Government and the prime object of all their endeavours. It is the reason why they have given ungrudging support to the League of Nations and why they have undertaken the burden of the guarantee embodied in the Locarno Treaty. The sole object of all these engagements is the elimination of war as an instrument of national policy, just as it is the purpose of the Peace Pact now proposed. It is because the object of both is the same that there is no real antagonism between the treaty engagements which His Majesty's Government have already accepted and the pact which is now proposed. The machinery of the Covenant and of the Treaty of Locarno, however, go somewhat further than a renunciation of war as a policy, in that they provide certain sanctions for a breach of their obligations. A clash might thus conceivably arise between the existing treaties and the proposed pact unless it is understood that the obligations of the new engagement will cease to operate in respect of a party which breaks its pledges and adopts hostile measures against one of its co-contractants.

9. For the Government of this country respect for the obligations arising out of the Covenant of the League of Nations and out of the Locarno Treaties is fundamental. Our position in this regard is identical with that of the German Government as indicated in their Note of April 27th. His Majesty's Government could not agree to any new treaty which would weaken or undermine these engagements on which the peace of Europe rests. Indeed, public interest in this country in the scrupulous fulfilment of these engagements is so great that His Majesty's Government would for their part prefer to see some such

provision as Article 4 of the French draft embodied in the text of the treaty. To this we understand there will be no objection. Mr. Kellogg has made it clear in the speech to which I have drawn attention that he had no intention by the terms of the new treaty of preventing the parties to the Covenant of the League or to the Locarno Treaty from fulfilling their obligations.

10. The language of Article 1, as to the renunciation of war as an instrument of national policy, renders it desirable that I should remind Your Excellency that there are certain regions of the world the welfare and integrity of which constitute a special and vital interest for our peace and safety. His Majesty's Government have been at pains to make it clear in the past that interference with these regions cannot be suffered. Their protection against attack is to the British Empire a measure of self-defence. It must be clearly understood that His Majesty's Government in Great Britain accept the new treaty upon the distinct understanding that it does not prejudice their freedom of action in this respect. The Government of the United States have comparable interests any disregard of which by a foreign Power they have declared that they would regard as an unfriendly act. His Majesty's Government believe, therefore, that in defining their position they are expressing the intention and meaning of the United States Government.

11. As regards the measure of participation in the new treaty before it would come into force, His Majesty's Government agree that it is not necessary to wait until all the nations of the world have signified their willingness to become parties. On the other hand, it would be embarrassing if certain States in Europe with whom the proposed participants are already in close treaty relations were not included among the parties. His Majesty's Government see no reason, however, to doubt that these States will gladly accept its terms. Universality would, in any case, be difficult of attainment, and might even be inconvenient, for there are some States whose Governments have not yet been universally recognized, and some which are scarcely in a position to ensure the maintenance of good order

and security within their territories. The conditions for the inclusion of such States among the parties to the new treaty is a question to which further attention may perhaps be devoted with advantage. It is, however, a minor question as compared with the attainment of the more important purpose in view.

12. After this examination of the terms of the proposed treaty and of the points to which it gives rise, Your Excellency will realize that His Majesty's Government find nothing in their existing commitments which prevents their hearty co-operation in this movement for strengthening the foundations of peace. They will gladly co-operate in the conclusion of such a pact as is proposed and are ready to engage with the interested Governments in the negotiations which are necessary for the purpose.

13. Your Excellency will observe that the detailed arguments in the foregoing paragraphs are expressed on behalf of His Majesty's Government in Great Britain. It will, however, be appreciated that the proposed treaty, from its very nature, is not one which concerns His Majesty's Government in Great Britain alone, but is one in which they could not undertake to participate otherwise than jointly and simultaneously with His Majesty's Governments in the Dominions and the Government of India. They have, therefore, been in communication with those Governments, and I am happy to be able to inform Your Excellency that as a result of the communications which have passed it has been ascertained that they are all in cordial agreement with the general principle of the proposed treaty. I feel confident, therefore, that on receipt of an invitation to participate in the conclusion of such a treaty they, no less than His Majesty's Government in Great Britain, will be prepared to accept the invitation.

I have, etc.,

AUSTEN CHAMBERLAIN.

XVI

REPLY OF THE JAPANESE GOVERNMENT

May 26, 1928.

I have the honour to acknowledge the receipt of Your Excellency's Note No. 336 of April 13th last, transmitting to me, under instructions from the Government of the United States, the preliminary draft of the proposed multi-lateral treaty representing in a general way the form of treaty which the Government of the United States are prepared to sign with the French, British, German, Italian, and Japanese Governments and any other Governments similarly disposed, with the object of securing the renunciation of war.

At the same time Your Excellency enclosed a copy of the correspondence recently exchanged between the Governments of the United States and the French Republic, commencing with a proposal put forward by M. Briand in June 1927; and you intimated that the Government of the United States desired to be informed whether the Japanese Government were in a position to give favourable consideration to the conclusion of such a treaty as that of which you enclosed a draft and, if not, what specific modifications in the text would make it acceptable.

I beg to inform Your Excellency that the Government of Japan sympathize warmly with the high and beneficent aims of the proposal now made by the United States, which they take to imply the entire abolition of the institution of war, and that they will be glad to render their most cordial cooperation towards the attainment of that end.

The proposal of the United States is understood to contain nothing that would refuse to independent States the right of self-defence, and nothing which is incompatible with the obligations of agreements guaranteeing the public peace, such as are embodied in the Covenant of the League of Nations and the Treaties of Locarno. Accordingly the Imperial Government firmly believe that unanimous agreement on a mutually acceptable text for such a treaty as is contemplated is well capable of realization by discussion between the six Powers referred to, and they would be happy to collaborate with cordial good will in the discussions with the purpose of securing what they are persuaded is the common desire of all the peoples of the world, namely, the cessation of wars and the definite establishment among the nations of an era of permanent and universal peace.

XVII

U.S. INVITATION TO THE DOMINIONS[1]

(Dated May 22nd and addressed to Sir Austen Chamberlain.)

SIR,

In the Note which you addressed to me on May 19, 1928, you were good enough to inform my Government that His Majesty's Government in Great Britain had been in communication with His Majesty's Governments in the Dominions and with the Government of India and had ascertained that they were all in cordial agreement with the general principle of the multi-lateral treaty for the renunciation of war which the Government of the United States proposed on April 13, 1928. You added that you felt confident, therefore, that His Majesty's Governments in the Dominions and the Government of India were prepared to accept an invitation to participate in the conclusion of such a treaty as that proposed by the Government of the United States.

I have been instructed to state to you that my Government has received this information with the keenest satisfaction. My Government has hoped from the outset of the present negotiations that the Governments of the Dominions and the Government of India would feel disposed to become parties to the suggested anti-war treaty. It is, moreover, most gratifying to the Government of the United States to learn that His Majesty's Governments in the Dominions and the Government of India are so favourably inclined towards the treaty for the renunciation of war which my Government proposed on April 13, 1928, as to wish to participate therein individually and as original signatories, and my Government, for its part, is most happy to accede to the suggestion contained in your Note to me of May 19, 1928.

Accordingly, I have been instructed to extend, through you, to His Majesty's Governments in Australia, New Zealand, and South Africa, and to the Government of India, a cordial

---

[1] From *The Times*, May 25, 1928.

invitation, in the name of the Government of the United States, to become original parties to the treaty for the renunciation of war which is now under consideration. Pursuant to my instructions, I also have the honour to inform you that the Government of the United States will address, through you, to His Majesty's Governments in Australia, New Zealand, and South Africa, and to the Government of India, at the same time and in the same manner as to the other Governments whose participation in the proposed treaty in the first instance is contemplated, any future communications which it may make on the subject of the treaty after it has been acquainted with the views of all the Governments to which its Note of April 13, 1928, was addressed.

I have, etc.

A. B. HOUGHTON.

XVIII

U.S. INVITATION TO THE IRISH FREE STATE

The following Note has been addressed to the Minister for External Affairs by the American Minister:—

DUBLIN,
May 22, 1928.

EXCELLENCY,

In the Note which he addressed to the American Ambassador at London on May 19, 1928, Sir Austen Chamberlain was good enough to inform my Government that His Majesty's Government in Great Britain had been in communication with His Majesty's Governments in the Dominions and with the Government of India and had ascertained that they were all in cordial agreement with the general principle of the multi-lateral treaty for the renunciation of war which the Government of the United States proposed on April 13, 1928. Sir Austen added that he felt confident therefore that His Majesty's Governments in the Dominions and the Government of India were prepared to accept an invitation to participate in the conclusion of such a treaty as that proposed by the Government of the United States.

I have been instructed to state to Your Excellency that my Government has received this information with the keenest satisfaction. My Government has hoped from the outset of the present negotiations that the Governments of the Dominions and the Government of India would feel disposed to become parties to the suggested anti-war treaty. It is, moreover, most gratifying to the Government of the United States to learn that His Majesty's Governments in the Dominions and the Government of India are so favourably inclined towards the treaty for the renunciation of war which my Government proposed on April 13, 1928, as to wish to participate therein individually and as original signatories, and my Government for its part is most happy to accede to the suggestion contained in Sir Austen Chamberlain's Note of May 19, 1928, to the American Ambassador at London.

Accordingly I have been instructed to extend to His Majesty's Government in the Irish Free State, in the name of the Government of the United States, a cordial invitation to become one of the original parties to the treaty for the renunciation of war which is now under consideration. Pursuant to my instructions, I also have the honour to inform you that the Government of the United States will address to His Majesty's Government in the Irish Free State, at the same time and in the same manner as to the other Governments whose participation in the proposed treaty in the first instance is contemplated, any future communications which it may make on the subject of the treaty after it has been acquainted with the views of all the Governments to which its Note of April 13, 1928, was addressed.

Accept, Excellency, the renewed assurance of my highest consideration.

REPLY OF THE IRISH FREE STATE GOVERNMENT[1]

May 30, 1928.

EXCELLENCY,

I have the honour to acknowledge receipt of Your Excellency's Note of May 22nd referring to the draft treaty for the renunciation of war and extending an invitation from your Government to the Government of the Irish Free State to become one of the original parties to the proposed treaty.

The Government of the Irish Free State warmly welcome the action of the United States Government in initiating this further advance towards the maintenance of general peace. They are in cordial agreement with the general principle of the draft treaty, which they confidently hope will ensure the peaceful settlement of future international disputes.

Sharing the view expressed by the Secretary of State of the United States in his speech before the American Society of International Law that nothing in the draft treaty is inconsistent with the Covenant of the League of Nations, the Government of the Irish Free State accept unreservedly the invitation of the United States Government to become a party to the treaty jointly with the other States similarly invited.

The Government of the Irish Free State will be glad, therefore, to participate in, and to further by every possible means, the negotiations which may be necessary for the conclusion of the pact.

Accept, Excellency, the renewed assurance of my highest consideration.

(*Signed*) P. McGILLIGAN.

HIS EXCELLENCY F. A. STERLING, Esq,
    Envoy Extraordinary and Minister Plenipotentiary
      of the United States of America,
        Dublin.

---

[1] From Official Record of the debate in the Dail, p. 2490.

NOTE FROM THE SECRETARY OF STATE FOR EXTERNAL
AFFAIRS, CANADA, TO THE UNITED STATES MINISTER
AT OTTAWA, IN REPLY TO THE MINISTER'S NOTE OF
MAY 22, 1928[1]

OFFICE OF THE SECRETARY OF STATE FOR
EXTERNAL AFFAIRS, CANADA, OTTAWA,
May 30, 1928.

SIR,

I have the honour to acknowledge your Note of May 22nd,
extending to His Majesty's Government in Canada, in the
name of the Government of the United States, an invitation
to become one of the original parties to the treaty for the
renunciation of war now under consideration.

The Government of Canada is certain that it speaks for the
whole Canadian people in welcoming the outcome, the proposed multi-lateral pact, of the discussion initiated almost a year
ago between the Governments of France and of the United
States. It is pleased to find that in this attitude it is in accord
with all His Majesty's other Governments. The proposals of
the United States Government, by their directness and simplicity, afford to the peoples of the world a new and notable
opportunity of ensuring lasting peace.

The Dominion of Canada, fortunate in its ties of kinship
and allegiance as well as in its historic and neighbourly
friendships, and with half a continent as its heritage, is less
exposed to the danger of attack or the temptation to aggression
than many other lands. Yet the Great War, with its burdens
of suffering and of loss, brought home the danger which all
countries share, and led Canada to turn with hope to the
efforts to build up effective barriers against war which took
shape in the League of Nations; it will welcome the present
proposals as a manifestation of the same striving for peace.

The question whether the obligations of the Covenant of the
League would conflict in any way with the obligations of

[1] From Canadian White Paper, p. 25.

the proposed pact has been given careful consideration. His Majesty's Government in Canada regards the League, with all its limitations, as an indispensable and continuing agency of international understanding, and would not desire to enter upon any course which would prejudice its effectiveness. It is, however, convinced that there is no conflict either in the letter or in the spirit between the Covenant and the multi-lateral pact, or between the obligations assumed under each.

The pre-eminent value of the League lies in its positive and preventive action. In bringing together periodically the representatives of fifty States, it builds up barriers against war by developing a spirit of conciliation, an acceptance of publicity in international affairs, a habit of co-operation in common ends, and a permanently available machinery for the adjustment of differences. It is true that the Covenant also contemplates the application of sanctions in the event of a member State going to war, if in so doing it has broken the pledges of the Covenant to seek a peaceful solution of disputes. Canada has always opposed any interpretation of the Covenant which would involve the application of these sanctions automatically or by the decision of other States. It was on the initiative of Canada that the Fourth Assembly, with a single negative vote, accepted the interpretative resolution to which the Secretary of State of the United States recently referred, indicating that it is for the constitutional authorities of each State to determine in what degree it is bound to assure the execution of the obligations of this Article by employment of its military forces. The question of sanctions has received further consideration by later Assemblies. It is plain that the full realization of the ideal of joint economic or military pressure upon an outlaw Power, upon which some of the founders of the League set great store, will require either an approach to the universality of the League contemplated when the Covenant was being drawn, or an adjustment of the old rules of neutrality to meet the new conditions of co-operative defence.

In any event, if, as would seem to be the case, the proposed multi-lateral treaty does not impose any obligation upon a signatory in relation to a State which has not signed the treaty or has broken it, any decision taken to apply sanctions against a member of the League which has made war in violation of its Covenant pledges would not appear to conflict with the obligations of the treaty.

His Majesty's Government in Canada will have pleasure in co-operating in any future negotiations with a view to becoming a signatory to a treaty such as is proposed by the Government of the United States in the invitation which it has extended, and to recommending its acceptance to the Canadian Parliament.

Accept, Sir, the renewed assurances of my highest consideration.

W. L. MACKENZIE KING,
Secretary of State for External Affairs.

The HONOURABLE WILLIAM PHILLIPS,
   Minister of the United States of America, Ottawa.

XXI

REPLY OF THE NEW ZEALAND GOVERNMENT[1]

Sir Austen Chamberlain to Mr. Atherton

FOREIGN OFFICE,
May 30, 1928

SIR,

In the Note which Mr. Houghton was so good as to address to me on May 22nd, he extended on behalf of the Government of the United States an invitation to His Majesty's Governments in the Commonwealth of Australia, New Zealand and in the Union of South Africa, as well as to the Government of India, to participate individually and as original signatories in the treaty for the renunciation of war which is now under consideration.

2. I now have the honour to inform you that His Majesty's Government in New Zealand have received with warm appreciation the invitation addressed to New Zealand to become an original party to the treaty proposed by the Government of the United States for the renunciation of war. His Majesty's Government in New Zealand welcome the opportunity, in co-operation with His Majesty's Governments in other parts of the British Empire, of associating themselves with the Government of the United States in this movement to add greater security to the peace of the world, and they will be happy to share in any negotiations leading to the conclusion of the proposed treaty.

I have, etc.,

AUSTEN CHAMBERLAIN.

[1] From *The Times*, June 1, 1928.

XXII

REPLY OF THE AUSTRALIAN GOVERNMENT[1]

Sir Austen Chamberlain to Mr. Atherton

FOREIGN OFFICE,
June 2, 1928.

SIR,

In the Note which Mr. Houghton was so good as to address to me on May 22nd last, he extended on behalf of the Government of the United States an invitation to His Majesty's Government in the Commonwealth of Australia to participate individually and as an original signatory in the treaty for the renunciation of war which is now under consideration.

2. I now have the honour to inform you that His Majesty's Government in the Commonwealth of Australia have received with appreciation the invitation to participate as an original party in the treaty for the renunciation of war which has been proposed by the Government of the United States of America. His Majesty's Government in the Commonwealth of Australia have carefully and sympathetically examined the draft treaty submitted to them together with the correspondence that has so far been exchanged between the interested Governments. They believe that a treaty such as that proposed would be a further material safeguard to the peace of the world, and they will be happy to co-operate to the fullest extent in its successful conclusion.

I have, etc.,

AUSTEN CHAMBERLAIN.

[1] From *The Times*, June 5, 1928.

XXIII

REPLY OF THE GOVERNMENT OF INDIA[1]

FOREIGN OFFICE, S.W. 1,
June 11, 1928.

SIR,

In the Note which Mr. Houghton was so good as to address to me on the 22nd ultimo, he extended, on behalf of the Government of the United States, an invitation to the Government of India to participate individually and as an original signatory in the treaty for the renunciation of war which is now under consideration.

2. I now have the honour to inform you that the Government of India have requested that an expression of their warm thanks may be conveyed to the United States Government for this invitation, which they are happy to accept. I have the honour to add that the Government of India desire to associate themselves with the Note which I had the honour to address to Mr. Houghton on the 19th ultimo.

I have, etc.,
(*For the Secretary of State*)
(*Signed*) R. L. CRAIGIE.

RAY ATHERTON, Esq.,
Chargé d'Affaires, London.

[1] From *The Times*, June 13, 1928.

XXIV

REPLY OF THE SOUTH AFRICAN GOVERNMENT[1]

FOREIGN OFFICE, S.W. 1,
June 15, 1928.

SIR,

With reference to the Note which Mr. Houghton was so good as to address to me on May 22nd conveying an invitation to His Majesty's Government in the Union of South Africa to become an original party to the proposed treaty for the renunciation of war, I have the honour to inform you that the following message has been received by telegraph from General Hertzog, Minister of External Affairs of the Union of South Africa, for communication to you:—

"Through the good offices of His Majesty's Government in the United Kingdom the contents of the Note addressed by your Excellency to his Excellency the British Secretary of State for Foreign Affairs on May 22nd were duly conveyed to me. On behalf of His Majesty's Government in the Union of South Africa I beg to state that the cordial invitation of the Government of the United States extended to His Majesty's Government in the Union of South Africa to participate individually and as an original signatory in the treaty for the renunciation of war which the United States Government proposed to various Governments on April 13th last, is highly appreciated and that His Majesty's Government in the Union of South Africa will gladly take part therein, as invited, together with the other Governments whose participation in the proposed treaty was invited in the first instance.

"In expressing their willingness to be a party to the proposed treaty His Majesty's Government in the Union of South Africa take it for granted—

"(*a*) that it is not intended to deprive any party to the proposed treaty of any of its natural right of legitimate self-defence;

"(*b*) that a violation by any one of the parties of any of the provisions of the proposed treaty will free the other parties from obligation to observe its terms in respect of the party committing such violation; and

"(*c*) that provision will be made for rendering it quite clear that it is not intended that the Union of South Africa, by becoming a party

---

[1] From *The Times*, June 16, 1928.

to the proposed treaty, would be precluded from fulfilling, as a member of the League of Nations, its obligations towards the other members thereof under the provisions of the Covenant of the League."

I have, etc.,
(*For the Secretary of State*)
(*Signed*)   R. L. CRAIGIE.

RAY ATHERTON, Esq.,
    Chargé d'Affaires, London.

XXV

EXTRACT FROM PRESIDENT COOLIDGE'S MEMORIAL DAY
SPEECH AT GETTYSBERG, U.S.A.[1]

May 30, 1928.

As is well known, we are also engaged in conversations with
different Powers for putting peace on a new basis and making
it still more permanent. In June 1927 M. Briand, the French
Minister of Foreign Affairs, made an historic proposal to this
Government. He suggested that France and the United States
sign a treaty condemning recourse to war and renouncing it as
an instrument of national policy in their mutual relations.
During the eleven months that have since elapsed, this suggestion has been developed into one of the most impressive peace
movements that the world has ever seen. The United States
has accepted the principle underlying M. Briand's suggestion
and has advocated its extension so as to include within the
scope of the proposed treaty not only France and the United
States, but also Great Britain, Germany, Italy, and Japan, and
any other nations of the world that might care to join with
these six Powers in a common renunciation of war.

In order to facilitate and to demonstrate that a treaty such
as that desired by the United States could be short, simple
and straightforward, Mr. Kellogg, Secretary of State, submitted
on April 13, 1928, for the consideration of the other interested
Powers a preliminary draft of a treaty representing in a general
way the form of treaty which he suggested we were prepared
to conclude. This draft treaty has met with very favourable
reception. Not only has the idea of a multi-lateral treaty for the
renunciation of war been endorsed by public opinion here and
abroad, but the Governments themselves have approached the
matter with an interest and a sympathy which are most
encouraging.

We have gathered to pay tribute to our soldier dead. This
day is consecrated to their memory. It seems to me that the
greatest honour that we can do to those who have died on the

[1] From *New York Herald and Tribune*, May 31, 1928.

field of battle that this Republic might live is soberly to pledge ourselves to bend our every effort to prevent any recurrence of war. The government of the people, by the people, for the people, which Lincoln described in his immortal address, is a government of peace, not of war, and our dead will not have died in vain if, inspired by their sacrifice, we endeavour by every means within our power to prevent the shedding of human blood in the attempted settlement of international controversies. It is my earnest hope that success may crown the negotiations now in progress, and that the ideals which have inspired the French Minister of Foreign Affairs and the Secretary of State of the United States in their joint efforts to find a solution of the problem of peace may find a practical realization in the early making of a multi-lateral treaty limiting future resort to war.

XXVI

EXTRACT FROM SPEECH DELIVERED BY HON. FRANK B. KELLOGG AT THE HOTEL PENNSYLVANIA, NEW YORK, ON JUNE 11, 1928, ON THE TERCENTENARY ANNIVERSARY OF THE FOUNDING OF THE FIRST REFORMED DUTCH CHURCH ON THE ISLAND OF MANHATTAN IN 1628

It is known to all of you that in June 1927 M. Briand, the French Minister for Foreign Affairs, made an historic proposal to the United States. He suggested that our two countries conclude a treaty condemning war and renouncing it as an instrument of national policy in their mutual relations. That proposal was carefully considered by the United States, and the more it was examined the more we were convinced that, to realize its greatest usefulness, M. Briand's inspiring idea should be enlarged so as to make it possible to bring within the scope of such a treaty not only France and the United States but also the other nations of the world. The French Government was informed of our views, and for several months we exchanged Notes with France on this general subject. Finally, on April 13, 1928, the United States, with the full approval of France, transmitted, for the consideration of the British, German, Italian, and Japanese Governments the texts of the diplomatic Notes previously exchanged by the two Governments. At the same time the United States submitted to those Governments on its own initiative a preliminary draft of a treaty for the renunciation of war, representing in a general way the form of treaty which it was prepared to sign. The four Governments addressed were asked whether they were in a position to conclude such a treaty.

Encouraging replies have now been received from them all. They have all expressed cordial approval of the principle underlying the proposal of the United States and have indicated a sincere desire to collaborate in the conclusion of an appropriate treaty for the renunciation of war. The British Government, in addition to informing the United States that it found it had no commitments which would prevent signing a treaty such as we suggested, indicated that the Dominion Governments and the Government of India would be glad to become original signatories of the treaty, and appropriate invitations were thereupon sent to the Governments of Canada, the Irish Free State, South Africa, Australia, New Zealand, and the Government of India. The replies which we have received demonstrate that the several Governments heartily endorse the plan and are ready and willing to join in the negotiation of a treaty such as that proposed by the United States. Other Governments have also informally indicated their desire to participate in a treaty for the renunciation of war, and I earnestly hope that we shall soon succeed in reaching an agreement as to the precise text to be employed. The force of public opinion in this country and abroad has already made itself felt. The peoples of the world seem unquestionably to want their Governments to renounce war in the most effective way possible.

The anti-war treaty which the United States has proposed and which, as I have said, has its origin in the suggestions made by M. Briand a year ago, is simple and straightforward. The grand conception of the French Foreign Secretary undoubtedly had its inspiration in the deep-seated desire of the French people, as well as all the people of Europe, to avoid another great cataclysm of war. It is significant that Europe, since the great war, has been engaged in efforts of various kinds to assuage national and racial animosities; to settle international disputes and to prevent war. What I believe, and I am convinced that the leaders of the Governments believe, is that there should be one more step in this effort, and that is a simple declaration against war as an instrument for the settlement of international controversies. Since this discussion commenced between France and the United States, the idea has appealed in increasing force to the public opinion of the world. As one looks back over the history of the four years of that unparalleled carnage which left its trail of desolation and death, one cannot believe that the nations will hesitate to commit themselves in the most unqualified and solemn terms to the renunciation of recourse to war.

There are, of course, cynical individuals who decry all efforts to lessen the likelihood of war and belittle in particular the present negotiations. There are others who believe in war as an institution and whose support, if any, will be cold and grudging; but I am convinced that those of us who believe wholeheartedly in this movement are no less realistic. We know that the peoples of the world desire peace and dread any new international conflict. We know that the peoples of the world are becoming more and more articulate and that Governments are becoming more and more responsive to their wishes. We now find peoples and Governments united in a common and sincere desire to prevent so far as possible the outbreak of any war anywhere and seriously considering the best form of multi-lateral treaty to give effect to their aspirations. It is a most impressive manifestation of the spiritual nature of man.

With the passage of time the emphasis in our present negotiations is being placed not on narrow technical considerations of a legalistic nature, but on the broad principles underlying the entire idea. It is peace, not war, that we are seeking to perpetuate, and I am firmly convinced that the simple straightforward unequivocal declaration against war which the United States borrowed from M. Briand and incorporated in its draft treaty is the one that has the greatest moral value and the one that will in the long run commend itself to all the peoples concerned. It has no hidden meaning. It is easily understood. The interpretation placed upon it by the United States has been publicly stated in the address which it was my privilege to deliver a few weeks ago before the American Society of International Law. The accuracy of this interpretation has been contested by no Government. On the contrary, many Governments have indicated that they agree with the conclusions set forth in that address. In these circumstances, is it too much to hope that all may find themselves in the near future able to sign with the United States a treaty under which we all declare, in the names of our respective peoples, that we condemn recourse to war for the solution of international controversies and renounce it as an instrument of national policy in our relations with one another, and agree that the settlement or solution of all disputes or conflicts, of whatever nature or of whatever origin they may be, which may arise among us shall never be sought except by pacific means? I do not think that it is too much to hope that such a treaty will be signed.

I am persuaded that the time has come when a frank renunciation of war as an instrument of national policy should be made to the end that the peaceful and friendly relations now existing between the peoples of the world may be perpetuated. I am convinced, moreover, that all changes in these relations should be sought only by pacific means and be the result of a peaceful and orderly process; and any nation which shall hereafter seek to promote its national interests by resort to war should be denied the benefits and guarantees furnished by the proposed treaty. This is the object of the negotiations in which fifteen world Powers are now engaged, and in the name of the Government of the United States I bespeak the continued support of this and every other Church in the present movement for the promotion of world peace.

KELLOGG.

MR. RAY ATHERTON, AMERICAN CHARGÉ D'AFFAIRES, TO SIR AUSTEN CHAMBERLAIN

LONDON,
June 23, 1928.

SIR,

It will be recalled that, pursuant to the understanding reached between the Government of France and the Government of the United States, the American Ambassadors at London, Berlin, Rome, and Tokio transmitted on April 13, 1928, to the Governments to which they were respectively accredited the text of M. Briand's original proposal of June 20, 1927, together with copies of the Notes subsequently exchanged by France and the United States on the subject of a multi-lateral treaty for the renunciation of war. At the same time the Government of the United States also submitted for consideration a preliminary draft of a treaty representing in a general way the form of treaty which it was prepared to sign and inquired whether the Governments thus addressed were in a position to give favourable consideration thereto. The text of the identic Notes of April 13, 1928, and a copy of the draft treaty transmitted therewith were also brought to the attention of the Government of France by the American Ambassador at Paris.

It will likewise be recalled that on April 20, 1928, the Government of the French Republic circulated among the other interested Governments, including the Government of the United States, an alternative draft treaty, and that, in an address which he delivered on April 28, 1928, before the American Society of International Law, the Secretary of State of the United States explained fully the construction placed by my Government upon the treaty proposed by it, referring as follows to the six major considerations emphasized by France in its alternative draft treaty and prior diplomatic correspondence with my Government:—

ONE: SELF-DEFENCE.

"There is nothing in the American draft of an anti-war treaty which restricts or impairs in any way the right of self-defence. That right is inherent in every sovereign State and is implicit in every treaty. Every nation is free at all times and regardless of treaty provisions to defend its territories from attack or invasion and it alone is competent to decide whether circumstances require recourse to war in self-defence. If it has a good case, the world will applaud and not condemn its action. Express recognition by treaty of this inalienable right, however, gives rise to the same difficulty encountered in any effort to define aggression. It is the identical question approached from the other side. In this respect, no treaty provision can add to the natural right of self-defence. It is not in the interest of peace that a treaty should stipulate a juristic conception of self-defence, since it is far too easy for the unscrupulous to mould events to accord with an agreed definition.

Two: The League Covenant.

" The Covenant imposes no affirmative primary obligation to go to war. The obligation, if any, is secondary and attaches only when deliberately accepted by a State. Article Ten of the Covenant has, for example, been interpreted, by a resolution submitted to the Fourth Assembly, but not formally adopted owing to one adverse vote, to mean that: 'It is for the constitutional authorities of each member to decide, in reference to the obligation of preserving the independence and the integrity of the territory of the members, in what degree the member is bound to assure the execution of this obligation by employment of its military forces.'

"There is, in my opinion, no necessary inconsistency between the Covenant and the idea of an unqualified renunciation of war. The Covenant can, it is true, be construed as authorizing war in certain circumstances, but it is an authorization and not a positive requirement.

Three: The Treaties of Locarno.

"If the parties to the Treaties of Locarno are under any positive obligation to go to war, such obligation certainly would not attach until one of the parties has resorted to war in violation of its solemn pledges thereunder. It is therefore obvious that, if all the parties to the Locarno Treaties become parties to the multi-lateral anti-war treaty proposed by the United States, there would be a double assurance that the Locarno Treaties would not be violated by recourse to arms. In such an event it would follow that resort to war by any State, in violation of the Locarno Treaties, would also be a breach of the multi-lateral anti-war treaty, and the other parties to the anti-war treaty would thus, as a matter of law, be automatically released from their obligations thereunder and free to fulfil their Locarno commitments. The United States is entirely willing that all parties to the Locarno Treaties should become parties to its proposed anti-war treaty, either through signature in the first instance, or by immediate accession to the treaty as soon as it comes into force in the manner provided in Article Three of the American draft, and it will offer no objection when and if such a suggestion is made.

FOUR: TREATIES OF NEUTRALITY.

"The United States is not informed as to the precise treaties which France has in mind, and cannot, therefore, discuss their provisions. It is not unreasonable to suppose, however, that the relations between France and the States whose neutrality she has guaranteed are sufficiently close and intimate to make it possible for France to persuade such States to adhere seasonably to the anti-war treaty proposed by the United States. If this were done, no party to the anti-war treaty could attack the neutralized States without violating the treaty and thereby automatically freeing France and the other Powers in respect of the treaty-breaking State from the obligations of the anti-war treaty. If the neutralized States were attacked by a State not a party to the anti-war treaty, the latter treaty would, of course, have no bearing and France would be as free to act under the treaties guaranteeing neutrality as if she were not a party to the anti-war treaty. It is difficult to perceive, therefore, how treaties guaranteeing neutrality can be regarded as necessarily preventing the conclusion by France or any other Power of a multi-lateral treaty for the renunciation of war.

FIVE: RELATIONS WITH A TREATY-BREAKING STATE.

"As I have already pointed out, there can be no question, as a matter of law, that violation of a multi-lateral anti-war treaty through resort to war by one party thereto would automatically release the other parties from their obligations to the treaty-breaking State. Any express recognition of this principle of law is wholly unnecessary.

SIX: UNIVERSALITY.

"From the beginning it has been the hope of the United States that its proposed multi-lateral anti-war treaty should be world-wide in its application, and appropriate provision therefore was made in the draft submitted to the other Governments on April 13th. From a practical standpoint, it is clearly preferable, however, not to postpone the coming into force of an anti-war treaty until all the nations of the world can agree upon the text of such a treaty and cause it to be ratified. For one reason or another, a State so situated as to be no menace to the peace of the world might obstruct agreement or delay ratification in such manner as to render abortive the efforts of all the other Powers. It is highly improbable, moreover, that a form of treaty acceptable to the British, French, German, Italian, and Japanese Governments, as well as to the United States, would not be equally acceptable to most if not all of the other Powers of the world. Even were this not the case, however, the coming into force among the above-named six Powers of an effective anti-war treaty and their observance thereof would be a practical guarantee against a second world war. This in itself would be a tremendous service to humanity, and the United States is not willing to jeopardize the practical success of the proposal which it has made by conditioning the coming into force of the treaty upon prior universal or almost universal acceptance."

The British, German, Italian, and Japanese Governments have now replied to my Government's Notes of April 13, 1928, and the Governments of the British Dominions and of India have likewise replied to the invitations addressed to them on May 22, 1928, by my Government, pursuant to the suggestion conveyed in the Note of May 19, 1928, from His Majesty's Government in Great Britain. None of these Governments has expressed any dissent from the above-quoted construction, and none has voiced the least disapproval of the principle underlying the proposal of the United States for the promotion of world peace. Neither has any of the replies received by the Government of the United States suggested any specific modification of the text of the draft treaty proposed by it on April 13, 1928, and my Government, for its part, remains convinced that no modification of the text of its proposal for a multi-lateral treaty for the renunciation of war is necessary to safeguard the legitimate interests of any nation. It believes that the right of self-defence is inherent in every sovereign State and implicit in every treaty. No specific reference to that inalienable attribute of sovereignty is therefore necessary or desirable. It is no less evident that resort to war, in violation of the proposed treaty by one of the parties thereto, would release the other parties from their obligations under the treaty towards the belligerent State. This principle is well recognized. So far as the Locarno Treaties are concerned, my Government has felt from the very first that participation in the anti-war treaty by the Powers which signed the Locarno Agreements, either through signature in the first instance or thereafter, would meet every practical requirement of the situation since, in such event, no State could resort to war in violation of the Locarno Treaties without simultaneously violating the anti-war treaty, thus leaving the other parties thereto free so far as the treaty-breaking State is concerned. As you know, the Government of the United States has welcomed the idea that all parties to the Treaties of Locarno should be among the original signatories of the proposed treaty for the renunciation of war, and provision therefor has been made in the draft treaty which I have the honour to transmit herewith. The same procedure would cover the treaties guaranteeing neutrality to which the Government of France has referred. Adherence to the proposed treaty by all parties to these other treaties would completely safeguard their rights, since subsequent resort to war by any of them or by any party to the anti-war treaty would violate the latter treaty as well as the neutrality treaty, and thus leave the other parties to the anti-war treaty free, so far as the treaty-breaking State is concerned. My Government would be entirely willing, however, to agree that the parties to such neutrality treaties should be original signatories of the multi-lateral anti-war treaty, and it has no reason to believe that such an arrangement would meet with any objection on the part of the other Governments now concerned in the present negotiations.

While my Government is satisfied that the draft treaty proposed by it on April 13, 1928, could be properly accepted by the Powers of the world without change, except for including among the original signatories the British Dominions, India, all parties to the Treaties of Locarno and, it may be, all parties to the neutrality treaties mentioned by the Government of France, it has no desire to delay or complicate the present negotiations by rigidly adhering to the precise phraseology of that draft, particularly since it appears that, by modifying the draft in form though not in substance, the points raised by other Governments can be satisfactorily met and general agreement upon the text of the treaty to be signed be promptly reached. The Government of the United States has therefore decided to submit to the fourteen other Governments now concerned in these negotiations a revised draft of a multi-lateral treaty for the renunciation of war. The text of this revised draft is identical with that of the draft proposed by the United States on April 13, 1928, except that the preamble now provides that the British Dominions, India, and all parties to the Treaties of Locarno are to be included among the Powers called upon to sign the treaty in the first instance, and except that

the first three paragraphs of the preamble have been changed
to read as follows :—

"Deeply sensible of their solemn duty to promote the welfare of
mankind;

"Persuaded that the time has come when a frank renunciation of
war as an instrument of national policy should be made to the end that
the peaceful and friendly relations now existing between their peoples
may be perpetuated;

"Convinced that all changes in their relations with one another should
be sought only by pacific means and be the result of a peaceful and
orderly process and that any signatory Power which shall hereafter
seek to promote its national interests by resort to war should be denied
the benefits furnished by this treaty."

The revised preamble thus gives express recognition to the
principle that, if a State resorts to war in violation of the
treaty, the other contracting parties are released from their
obligations under the treaty to that State. It also provides for
participation in the treaty by all parties to the Treaties of
Locarno, thus making it certain that resort to war, in violation
of the Locarno Treaties, would also violate the present treaty
and release not only the other signatories of the Locarno
Treaties but also the other signatories to the anti-war treaty
from their obligations to the treaty-breaking State. Moreover,
as stated above, my Government would be willing to have
included among the original signatories the parties to the
neutrality treaties referred to by the Government of the
French Republic, although it believes that the interests of those
States would be adequately safeguarded if, instead of signing
in the first instance, they should choose to adhere to the treaty.

In these circumstances, I have the honour to transmit
herewith, for the consideration of His Majesty's Government in
Great Britain and Northern Ireland, for the consideration of
His Majesty's Governments in the Commonwealth of Australia,
New Zealand, and the Union of South Africa as well as for
the consideration of the Government of India, a draft of a
multi-lateral treaty for the renunciation of war, containing the
changes outlined above. I have been instructed to state in this
connection that the Government of the United States is ready

to sign at once a treaty in the form herein proposed, and to express the fervent hope that His Majesty's Government in Great Britain and Northern Ireland and also His Majesty's Governments in the Commonwealth of Australia, New Zealand, and the Union of South Africa, as well as the Government of India, will be able promptly to indicate their readiness to accept without qualification or reservation the form of treaty now suggested by the United States.

If the Governments of Australia, Belgium, Canada, Czecho-Slovakia, France, Germany, Great Britain, India, the Irish Free State, Italy, Japan, New Zealand, Poland, South Africa, and the United States can now agree to conclude this anti-war treaty among themselves, my Government is confident that the other nations of the world will, as soon as the treaty comes into force, gladly adhere thereto, and that this simple procedure will bring mankind's agelong aspirations for universal peace nearer to practical fulfilment than ever before in the history of the world.

I have the honour to state, in conclusion, that the Government of the United States would be pleased to be informed at as early a date as may be convenient whether His Majesty's Government in Great Britain and Northern Ireland, His Majesty's Governments in the Commonwealth of Australia, New Zealand, and the Union of South Africa, as well as the Government of India, are willing to join with the United States and other similarly disposed Governments in signing a definitive treaty for the renunciation of war in the form transmitted herewith.

I have the honour to be,
with the highest consideration,
Sir,
Your most obedient,
humble servant,
RAY ATHERTON,
Chargé d'Affaires ad interim.

THE RIGHT HON. SIR AUSTEN CHAMBERLAIN, K.G.,
Foreign Office, S.W.1.

Enclosure:
Draft of proposed Treaty.

DRAFT OF PROPOSED TREATY

The President of the United States of America;

The President of the French Republic;

His Majesty the King of the Belgians;

The President of the Czecho-Slovak Republic;

His Majesty the King of Great Britain, Ireland, and the British Dominions beyond the Seas, Emperor of India;

The President of the German Reich;

His Majesty the King of Italy;

His Majesty the Emperor of Japan;

The President of the Republic of Poland;

Deeply sensible of their solemn duty to promote the welfare of mankind;

Persuaded that the time has come when a frank renunciation of war as an instrument of national policy should be made, to the end that the peaceful and friendly relations now existing between their peoples may be perpetuated;

Convinced that all changes in their relations with one another should be sought only by pacific means and be the result of a peaceful and orderly process and that any signatory Power which shall hereafter seek to promote its national interests by resort to war should be denied the benefits furnished by this treaty;

Hopeful that, encouraged by their example, all the other nations of the world will join in this humane endeavour and, by adhering to the present treaty as soon as it comes into force, bring their peoples within the scope of its beneficent provisions, thus uniting the civilized nations of the world in a common renunciation of war as an instrument of their national policy;

Have decided to conclude a treaty and for that purpose have appointed as their respective plenipotentiaries:

The President of the United States of America;

The President of the French Republic;

His Majesty the King of the Belgians;

The President of the Czecho-Slovak Republic;

His Majesty the King of Great Britain, Ireland, and the British Dominions beyond the Seas, Emperor of India;

For Great Britain and Northern Ireland and all parts of the British Empire which are not separate members of the League of Nations;

For the Dominion of Canada;

For the Commonwealth of Australia;

For the Dominion of New Zealand;

For the Union of South Africa·

For the Irish Free State;

For India;

The President of the German Reich;
His Majesty the King of Italy;
His Majesty the Emperor of Japan;
The President of the Republic of Poland;
Who, having communicated to one another their full powers, found in good and due form, have agreed upon the following articles:—

Article I.

The High Contracting Parties solemnly declare, in the names of their respective peoples, that they condemn recourse to war for the solution of international controversies, and renounce it as an instrument of national policy in their relations with one another.

Article II.

The High Contracting Parties agree that the settlement or solution of all disputes or conflicts, of whatever nature or of whatever origin they may be, which may arise among them, shall never be sought except by pacific means.

Article III.

The present treaty shall be ratified by the High Contracting Parties named in the preamble in accordance with their respective constitutional requirements, and shall take effect as between them as soon as all their several instruments of ratification shall have been deposited at . . .

This treaty shall, when it has come into effect as prescribed in the preceding paragraph, remain open as long as may be necessary for adherence by all the other Powers of the world. Every instrument evidencing the adherence of a Power shall be deposited at . . . and the treaty shall, immediately upon such deposit, become effective as between the Power thus adhering and the other Powers parties thereto.

It shall be the duty of the Government of . . . to furnish each Government named in the preamble, and every Government subsequently adhering to this treaty, with a certified copy of the treaty and of every instrument of ratification or adherence. It shall also be the duty of the Government of . . . telegraphically to notify such Governments immediately upon the deposit with it of each instrument of ratification or adherence.

In faith whereof the respective plenipotentiaries have signed this treaty in the French and English languages, both texts having equal force, and hereunto affixed their seals.

Done at . . . the . . . day of . . . in the Year of Our Lord one thousand nine hundred and twenty- . . .

THE TEXT OF THE REPLY OF THE GERMAN GOVERNMENT

BERLIN,
July 11, 1928.

MR. AMBASSADOR,

I beg to acknowledge the receipt of your Excellency's Note of June 23, 1928, concerning the conclusion of an international pact for the outlawry of war, and I have the honour, on behalf of the German Government, to make the following reply:—.

The German Government has examined with the greatest attention the contents of the Note and of the enclosed revised draft of the pact. It notes with satisfaction that the point of view adopted by the Government of the United States in the Note conforms with the fundamental view of the German Government as it was communicated in its Note of April 27, 1928. The German Government is also in agreement with the changes in the preamble of the draft of the pact. It is pleased, therefore, to be able to declare that it takes cognizance of the explanation of the Government of the United States contained in Your Excellency's Note of June 23, 1928, that it agrees with the interpretation, which is given in it, to the provisions of the proposed pact, and it is, in consequence, ready to sign this pact in its present proposed form.

Accept, Mr. Ambassador, the assurance of my marked esteem.

(*Signed*)   SCHUBERT.

REPLY OF THE FRENCH GOVERNMENT[1]

PARIS,
July 14, 1928.

MONSIEUR L'AMBASSADEUR,

In your letter of June 23rd last Your Excellency was kind enough to submit to me the revised text of the proposed treaty for the renunciation of war, accompanied by a Note containing the interpretation which the Government of the United States wishes to give to it.

I beg you to be kind enough to inform the Government of the United States with what interest the Government of the Republic has taken cognizance of this new communcation, intended to facilitate the signature of a treaty which both the French and the American peoples have so much at heart.

It follows from the new preamble that the proposed treaty indeed aims at the perpetuation of the pacific and friendly relations under the contractual conditions in which they are to-day established between the interested nations; that it is essentially a question for the signatory Powers of renouncing war "as an instrument of their national policy"; and also that the signatory Power which hereafter might seek by means of war to promote its own national interests should be denied the benefits of the treaty. The French Government is happy to declare that it is in agreement with these new stipulations, and takes note of the interpretations which the Government of the United States gives to the new treaty with a view to satisfying the various observations which had been formulated from the French point of view. These interpretations may be summarized as follows:—

Nothing in the new treaty restrains or compromises in any way the right of self-defence. Each nation will always remain free to defend its territory against attack or invasion; it alone is competent to decide whether circumstances require recourse to war in self-defence.

[1] From *The Times*. July 17, 1928.

Secondly, the new treaty is in opposition neither to the Covenant of the League of Nations, nor to the Locarno Treaties, nor the treaties of neutrality. Moreover, any violation of the new treaty by one of the contracting Powers would automatically release the other contracting Powers from their obligations towards the treaty-breaking State.

Finally, the signature which the Government of the United States has now offered to all the Powers signatory of the Locarno Treaties and is disposed to offer to all Powers parties to a treaty of neutrality is of a nature to give the new treaty that character of generality which accords with the views of the French Government.

In view of the provisions of the new preamble and the interpretations given to the treaty, the French Government finds that the new convention is compatible with the obligations of existing treaties to which France is a contracting party. In these circumstances the French Government is happy to be able to declare to the Government of the United States that it is now ready to sign the treaty.

At the moment of assuring its contribution to the realization of a project which is at length mature and the moral significance of which it has, since its inception, keenly appreciated, the Government of the Republic wishes to pay homage to the noble spirit with which the Government of the United States has envisaged this fresh manifestation of human fraternity, which conforms in the highest degree with the lofty aspirations of the French as of the American people and responds to the feeling of international solidarity, which is spreading more and more among the peoples of the world.

Accept, etc.,

BRIAND.

XXX

REPLY OF IRISH FREE STATE

July 14, 1928.

EXCELLENCY,

Your Excellency's Note of June 23rd enclosing a revised draft of the proposed treaty for the renunciation of war has been carefully studied by the Government of the Irish Free State.

As I informed you in my Note of May 30th, the Government of the Irish Free State were prepared to accept unreservedly the draft treaty proposed by your Government on April 13th, holding, as they did, that neither their right of self-defence, nor their commitments under the Covenant of the League of Nations, were in any way prejudiced by its terms.

The draft treaty as revised is equally acceptable to the Government of the Irish Free State, and I have the honour to inform you that they are prepared to sign it in conjunction with such other Governments as may be so disposed. As the effectiveness of the proposed treaty as an instrument for the suppression of war depends to a great extent upon its universal application, the Government of the Irish Free State hope that the treaty may meet with the approbation of the other Governments to whom it has been sent and that it may subsequently be accepted by all the other Powers of the world.

Accept, Excellency, the renewed assurance of my highest consideration.

HIS EXCELLENCY F. A. STERLING, Esq.,
Envoy Extraordinary and Minister Plenipotentiary of the
United States of America,
Legation of the United States of America, Dublin.

XXXI

THE ITALIAN GOVERNMENT'S REPLY

The Italian Government's reply, addressed to the United States Ambassador, July 15th, by Signor Mussolini, is as follows:—

"The Royal Government, which has carefully examined the last draft treaty for the outlawry of war proposed by the United States, takes cognizance of and agrees with the interpretation given by the United States to the same treaty in its Note of June 23rd, and with such premises declares itself willing to sign."

BELGIAN ACCEPTANCE[1]

BRUSSELS,
July 18, 1928.

Belgium's acceptance of Mr. Kellogg's Peace Pact proposals is contained in the following letter sent by M. Hymans, Foreign Minister, to Mr. Gibson, the United States Ambassador in Brussels:—

His Majesty's Government has examined with the greatest pleasure the letter dated June 23rd last, in which Your Excellency, acting on the instructions of your Government, invited Belgium to conclude a pluri-lateral treaty by which the High Contracting Parties would renounce war as an instrument of national policy. Belgium is devoted to peace, and she has always striven for the success of all attempts to establish it. Belgium is therefore happy to render homage to the ideal which inspires this proposed treaty, and the text drawn up by Washington meets with the complete approval of His Majesty's Government.

His Majesty's Government notes with satisfaction the explanations and interpretations of the treaty contained in Your Excellency's letter, and observes with pleasure that the proposed treaty will maintain in their entirety the rights and obligations imposed by the Covenant of the League of Nations and by the Locarno Treaties, which are fundamental guarantees of Belgium's security.

The Belgian Government greatly appreciates this action of the United States Government, by which the latter takes a share in the great work of encouraging the spirit of peace throughout the world and diminishing the danger of disasters in the future. His Majesty's Government would be obliged if the United States Government would inform it of the date and place chosen by the United States Government for the signature of the proposed treaty.

[1] From *Manchester Guardian*, July 19, 1928.

ACCEPTANCE OF POLISH GOVERNMENT

WARSAW,
July 17, 1928.

The following Note, indicating Poland's acceptance of Mr. Kellogg's proposals for a pact to outlaw war, has been communicated by the Polish Foreign Minister to the United States Minister in Warsaw:—

I have the honour to acknowledge the receipt of the Note which you were so good as to communicate to me on June 23rd, and to which was attached the proposal for a multi-lateral pact against war proposed by Mr. Kellogg. The principles which Mr. Kellogg has embodied in the above-mentioned proposal being entirely in conformity with the ends which Poland never ceases to pursue in her foreign policy, I have the honour to inform you that the Polish Government accepts the text of the aforesaid pact and declares itself ready to affix its signature thereto.

As regards the interpretation of the pact which you were good enough to give in your Note of June 23rd, and which affirms that the pact must assure the consolidation of pacific relations between States on the basis of existing international obligations, the Polish Government draws attention to the following points:—

1. That the pact does not affect the legitimate right of self-defence possessed by each State.

2. That any State which, after signing the pact, attempts to further its national interests by means of war will be deprived of the benefits of the pact.

3. That there is no conflict between the stipulations of the pact against war and the obligations of the Covenant of the League of Nations for States members of the League.

This statement springs from the fact that the pact proposed by Mr. Kellogg stipulates the renunciation of war as an instrument of national policy. The explanations given above, and the opportunity given to all States to join in the pact, are such as to assure to Poland the means of satisfying her international obligations. The Polish Government takes the liberty to express the hope of seeing in the near future the successful outcome of this great and joint work of peace and consolidation which is destined to confer its benefits upon the whole of humanity.

XXXIV

ACCEPTANCE OF BRITISH GOVERNMENT[1]

Sir Austen Chamberlain to Mr. Atherton

FOREIGN OFFICE,
July 18, 1928.

SIR,

I am happy to be able to inform you that after carefully studying the Note which you left with me on June 23rd, transmitting the revised text of the draft of the proposed treaty for the renunciation of war, His Majesty's Government in Great Britain accept the proposed treaty in the form transmitted by you and will be glad to sign it at such time and place as may be indicated for the purpose by the Government of the United States.

My Government have read with interest the explanations contained in your Note as to the meaning of the draft treaty, and also the comments which it contains upon the considerations advanced by other Powers in the previous diplomatic correspondence.

You will remember that in my previous communication of May 19th I explained how important it was to my Government that the principle should be recognized that if one of the parties to this proposed treaty resorted to war in violation of its terms, the other parties should be released automatically from their obligations towards that party under the treaty. I also pointed out that respect for the obligations arising out of the Covenant of the League of Nations and of the Locarno Treaties was the foundation of the policy of the Government of this country, and that they could not agree to any new treaty which would weaken or undermine these engagements.

The stipulation now inserted in the preamble under which any signatory Power hereafter seeking to promote its national interests by resort to war against another signatory is to be

[1] See British White Paper, Cmd. 3153.

denied the benefits furnished by the treaty is satisfactory to my Government, and is sufficient to meet the first point mentioned in the preceding paragraph.

His Majesty's Government in Great Britain do not consider, after mature reflection, that the fulfilment of the obligations which they have undertaken in the Covenant of the League of Nations and in the Treaty of Locarno is precluded by their acceptance of the proposed treaty. They concur in the view enunciated by the German Government in their Note of April 27th that those obligations do not contain anything which could conflict with the treaty proposed by the United States Government.

My Government have noted with peculiar satisfaction that all the parties to the Locarno Treaty are now invited to become original signatories of the new treaty, and that it is clearly the wish of the United States Government that all members of the League should become parties either by signature or accession. In order that as many States as possible may participate in the new movement, I trust that a general invitation will be extended to them to do so.

As regards the passage in my Note of May 19th relating to certain regions of which the welfare and integrity constitute a special and vital interest for our peace and safety, I need not repeat that His Majesty's Government in Great Britain accept the new treaty upon the understanding that it does not prejudice their freedom of action in this respect.

I am entirely in accord with the views expressed by Mr. Kellogg in his speech of April 28th that the proposed treaty does not restrict or impair in any way the right of self-defence, as also with his opinion that each State alone is competent to decide when circumstances necessitate recourse to war for that purpose.

In the light of the foregoing explanations, His Majesty's Government in Great Britain are glad to join with the United States and with all other Governments similarly disposed in signing a definitive treaty for the renunciation of war in the form transmitted in your Note of June 23rd. They rejoice to be associated with the Government of the United States of America and the other parties to the proposed treaty in a further and signal advance in the outlawry of war.

I have, etc.,

AUSTEN CHAMBERLAIN.

XXXV

ACCEPTANCES OF THE NEW ZEALAND, SOUTH AFRICAN, AND AUSTRALIAN GOVERNMENTS AND OF THE GOVERNMENT OF INDIA

ACCEPTANCE OF THE NEW ZEALAND GOVERNMENT

Sir Austen Chamberlain to Mr. Ray Atherton

FOREIGN OFFICE,
July 18, 1928.

SIR,

In the Note which you were so good as to address to me on June 23rd last you stated that the Government of the United States would be glad to be informed whether His Majesty's Government in New Zealand were willing to join with the United States and other similarly disposed Governments in signing a definitive treaty for the renunciation of war in the form of the draft treaty enclosed in your Note.

2. I now beg leave to inform you that His Majesty's Government in New Zealand desire to associate themselves with the terms of the Note which I have had the honour to address to you to-day notifying you of the willingness of His Majesty's Government in Great Britain to sign a multi-lateral treaty for the renunciation of war, as proposed by the Government of the United States. His Majesty's Government in New Zealand desire me to add that they will have the utmost satisfaction, in co-operation with His Majesty's Governments in other parts of the British Empire, in joining with the Government of the United States and with all other Governments similarly disposed in signing a treaty in the form proposed.

I have, etc.,
AUSTEN CHAMBERLAIN.

ACCEPTANCE OF THE SOUTH AFRICAN GOVERNMENT

Sir Austen Chamberlain to Mr. Ray Atherton

FOREIGN OFFICE,
July 18, 1928.

SIR,

In the Note which you were so good as to address to me on June 23rd last you stated that the Government of the United States would be glad to be informed whether His Majesty's Government in the Union of South Africa were willing to join with the United States and other similarly disposed Governments in signing a definitive treaty for the renunciation of war in the form of the draft treaty enclosed in your Note.

2. I now beg leave to inform you that the following message has been received by telegraph from General Hertzog, Minister of External Affairs of the Union of South Africa, for communication to you:—

"On behalf of His Majesty's Government in the Union of South Africa I have the honour to inform you that my Government have given their most serious consideration to the new draft treaty for the renunciation of war, submitted in your Note of June 23rd, and to the observations accompanying it.

"My Government note with great satisfaction (*a*) that it is common cause that the right of legitimate self-defence is not affected by the terms of the new draft; (*b*) that, according to the preamble, any signatory who shall seek to promote its national interests by resort to war shall forfeit the benefits of the treaty; and (*c*) that the treaty is open to accession by all Powers of the world.

"My Government have further examined the question whether the provisions of the present draft are inconsistent with the terms of the Covenant of the League of Nations by which they are bound, and have come to the conclusion that this is not the case, and that the objects which the League of Nations was constituted to serve can but be promoted by members of the League of Nations participating in the proposed treaty.

"His Majesty's Government in the Union of South Africa have, therefore, very great pleasure in expressing their willingness to sign, together with all other Powers which might be similarly inclined, the treaty in the form proposed in your Note under reference."

I have, etc.,

AUSTEN CHAMBERLAIN.

ACCEPTANCE OF THE GOVERNMENT OF INDIA

Sir Austen Chamberlain to Mr. Ray Atherton

FOREIGN OFFICE,
July 18, 1928.

SIR,

In the Note which you were so good as to address to me on June 23rd last you stated that the Government of the United States would be glad to be informed whether the Government of India were willing to join with the United States and other similarly disposed Governments in signing a definitive treaty for the renunciation of war in the form of the draft treaty enclosed in your Note.

2. I now beg leave to inform you that the Government of India associate themselves wholeheartedly and most gladly with the terms of the Note which I have had the honour to address to you to-day notifying you of the willingness of His Majesty's Government in Great Britain to sign a multilateral treaty for the renunciation of war as proposed by the Government of the United States.

I have, etc.,
AUSTEN CHAMBERLAIN.

ACCEPTANCE OF THE AUSTRALIAN GOVERNMENT

Sir Austen Chamberlain to Mr. Ray Atherton

FOREIGN OFFICE,
July 18, 1928.

SIR,

In the Note which you were so good as to address to me on June 23rd last you stated that the Government of the United States would be glad to be informed whether His Majesty's Government in the Commonwealth of Australia were willing to join with the United States and other similarly disposed Governments in signing a definitive treaty for the renunciation of war in the form of the draft treaty enclosed in your Note.

2. I now beg leave to inform you that His Majesty's Government in the Commonwealth of Australia have given the most careful consideration to your Note above mentioned and to the revised draft treaty which accompanied it, and that they accept the assurance given by the United States Secretary of State that the right of self-defence of a signatory State will not be impaired in any way by acceptance of the proposed treaty.

3. The Commonwealth Government have further observed that it is stated in your Note of June 23rd that the preamble to the revised treaty accords express recognition to the principle that, if one signatory State resorts to war in violation of the treaty, the other signatory States will be released from their obligations under the treaty to that State. They accept this declaration that the preamble in this respect is to be taken as a part of the substantive provisions of the treaty itself.

4. They have also particularly examined the draft treaty from the point of view of its relationship to the Covenant of the League of Nations, and in this connection have come to the conclusion that it is not inconsistent with the latter instrument.

5. His Majesty's Government in the Commonwealth of Australia add that the foregoing are the only questions to which the proposed treaty gives rise in which they are especially interested. As the text of the treaty which has now been submitted is completely satisfactory to them so far as these specific points are concerned, they will be quite agreeable to signing it in its present form.

I have, etc.,

AUSTEN CHAMBERLAIN.

ACCEPTANCE OF THE CANADIAN GOVERNMENT[1]

Mr. Mackenzie King to Mr. Kellogg

July 19, 1928.

I desire to acknowledge your Note of June 23rd and the revised draft which it contained of a treaty for the renunciation of war, and to state that His Majesty's Government in Canada cordially accepts the treaty as revised and is prepared to participate in its signature.

[1] See *The Times,* July 20, 1928.

ACCEPTANCE OF THE CZECHO-SLOVAK GOVERNMENT

PRAGUE,
July 20, 1928.

MONSIEUR LE MINISTRE,

I had the honour of receiving your Excellency's letter of June 23rd containing the invitation of the Government of the United States to the Government of the Republic of Czecho-Slovakia to sign the proposed treaty for the renunciation of war. The same invitation had been handed to our representative at Washington. The letter contains, in addition to the full text of the proposed treaty, a commentary upon the text which explains the attitude of the United States Government with regard to the observations made by the French Government and indicates in detail the meaning and significance which the Government of the United States wishes to give to the multilateral treaty in the event of the treaty being signed, ratified, and put into force.

I have the honour to present to your Excellency with this Note, the reply of the Czecho-Slovak Government :—

1. In the first place I wish to express my gratitude to the Government of the United States for the invitation which it has extended to us. From their initiation, we have followed the negotiations between the French Government and the Government of the United States, on the subject of a pact for the renunciation of war, with the greatest sympathy and attention and have been ready at any moment to associate ourselves with this noble project, which will mark a memorable date in the history of the world since the war.

In the negotiations which I have had the honour to carry on during the last months with the representatives of the United States, France, and Great Britain, I have repeatedly stressed the importance of this act and the political necessity of associating other Powers in it, and particularly those who assumed certain obligations in their negotiations at Locarno in 1925. The Government of the United States, in sympathy with this view, has recognized with the other Powers the justness of this claim and has addressed the invitation to us. The Czecho-Slovak Government regards this act as one of considerable political importance and warmly thanks the Government of Washington for it.

2. It is quite clear from the negotiations, preliminary to the signature of the treaty, as well as from the modifications of the original text, which have been effected in the preamble, and the explanations contained in the letter of your Government of June 23, 1928, that nothing in the treaty is incompatible either with the provisions of the Covenant of the League of Nations or with those of the treaties of Locarno or of the treaties of neutrality, or generally with the engagements contained in the treaties which have been contracted up to the present time.

3. It is clear also from the explanations given in Your Excellency's letter that any violation of the multi-lateral treaty by one of the contracting parties will fully liberate the other Powers, signatory to the treaty, from their obligations to the Power which shall have violated its engagements under the same treaty; it is clear also that the right of self-defence is in no way affected or restricted by the engagements of the new treaty, and that each Power remains entirely free to defend itself as it wills and so far as is necessary against an attack or an invasion by a foreign Power.

4. Thus defined, whether in the text of the preamble or in the detailed explanations contained in Your Excellency's letter, the new treaty has, in the view of the Government of the Czecho-Slovak Republic, as its object the consolidation and main-tenance of peaceful relations and friendly collaboration in the contractual conditions as they are established to-day between the nations interested in the treaty. In signing it the contracting parties renounce war as an instrument of their national policy and as the means of satisfying their selfish interests. This should be an immense benefit to humanity, and the Govern-ment of the Czecho-Slovak Republic is happy to see that the

Government of the United States is prepared to open the treaty to the adherence, on the one hand, of the Powers parties to the neutrality treaties, and on the other hand to all the other Powers, with the object of giving to the treaty as far as possible the character of universality.

5. The Government of the Czecho-Slovak Republic, having taken cognizance of the contents of Your Excellency's Note, formulates its view in the manner set forth above, thus accepting the explanations contained in your Note of June 23, 1928. It is extremely happy to be able to reply in the affirmative to the invitation of the Government of Washington, and while thanking it afresh most particularly for the noble efforts which it has made in the work of consolidating the peace of the world, declares that it is now prepared to sign the multi-lateral treaty in accordance with the proposal made by his Excellency, Mr. Kellogg, and contained in Your Excellency's letter of June 23, 1928.

May I add that the Government of the Czecho-Slovak Republic hastens to associate itself with all those who have already paid homage to the noble manifestation of the desire of the United States Government for the peace of the world, and that the foreign policy of our country sees in it the realization of the objects pursued by it during the past ten years.

Accept, etc.,

(*Signed*)   DR. EDWARD BENEŠ.

HIS EXCELLENCY M. LEWIS EINSTEIN,
    Envoy Extraordinary and Minister Plenipotentiary
        of the United States at Prague.

XXXVIII

TEXT OF THE NOTE HANDED BY THE JAPANESE FOREIGN MINISTER TO THE AMERICAN CHARGÉ D'AFFAIRES IN TOKIO ON JULY 20, 1928

I have the honour to acknowledge the receipt of your Note of the 23rd ultimo in which you recall to my attention your Government's identic Note of April 13th of this year, enclosing, together with certain correspondence, the preliminary draft of a treaty, and inquiring whether this Government were in a position to give favourable consideration to the latter. Your Note under reply further recalls that on April 20th the Government of the French Republic circulated among the interested Governments an alternative draft treaty, and that on April 28th the Secretary of State of the United States of America explained fully the construction placed by that Government on their own draft, in view of the matter emphasized in the French alternative.

You then transmit for the consideration of this Government the revised draft of a multi-lateral treaty, which takes in the British self-governing Dominions, India, and all parties to the Locarno Treaties, as original parties, and in the preamble of which is included a statement which is directed to recognizing the principle that if a State goes to war in violation of the treaty, the other contracting Powers are released from their obligations under the treaty to that State. Such a multi-lateral treaty as so revised, you are instructed to state your Government are ready to sign at once, and you express the fervent hope that this Government will be able promptly to indicate their readiness to accept it in this form without qualification or reservation.

You conclude by expressing the desire of the Government of the United States to know whether my Government are prepared to join with the United States and other similarly disposed Governments in signing a definitive treaty in the form so transmitted.

You now further inform me that the British, German, and Italian Governments have replied to your Government's Notes of April 13th last, and that the Governments of the British self-governing Dominions and of India have likewise replied to invitations addressed to them on the suggestion of His Britannic Majesty's Government in Great Britain; and you observe that none of these Governments has expressed any dissent from the constructions above referred to, or any disapproval of the principle underlying the proposals, nor have they suggested any specific modification of the text of the draft; and you proceed to reinforce in detail the explanations made by the Secretary of State in his speech of April 28th.

In reply, I have the honour to inform you that the Japanese Government are happy to be able to give their full concurrence to the alterations now proposed, their understanding of the original draft submitted to them in April last being, as I intimated in my Note to his Excellency Mr. MacVeagh, dated May 26, 1928, substantially the same as that entertained by the Government of the United States. They are, therefore, ready to give instructions for the signature, on that footing, of the treaty in the form in which it is now proposed. I cannot conclude without congratulating your Government most warmly upon the rapid and general acceptance which their proposals have met with.

The Imperial Government are proud to be among the first to be associated with a movement so plainly in unison with the hopes everywhere entertained, and confidently concur in the high probability of the acceptance of this simple and magnanimous treaty by the whole civilized world.

XXXIX

OFFICIAL ENGLISH TRANSLATION OF THE SPEECH
DELIVERED BY M. BRIAND ON THE OCCASION OF THE
SIGNATURE OF THE PACT IN PARIS, AUGUST 27, 1928

GENTLEMEN,

I am fully conscious that silence would best befit such a
solemn occasion. What I should like, without any further words,
would be to let each of you simply rise from his seat to go and
affix his signature, in the name of his own country, to the
greatest collective deed born of peace. But I should be failing
in my duty to my country if I did not tell you how deeply it
feels the honour of welcoming the first signatories of the General
Pact for the Renunciation of War.

If this honour has been left to France, as an acknowledg-
ment of the moral standing she enjoys thanks to her constant
efforts in the cause of peace, I gladly accept such a tribute on
behalf of the Government of the French Republic, and I express
the gratification of a whole people, happy that the inmost
recesses of their national psychology should at last be understood by the world.

While extending to you, gentlemen, a cordial welcome, let
me rejoice at seeing gathered here, save those who were
unavoidably prevented from coming by their state of health
or by their other duties, all the statesmen who, in their capacity
of Ministers for Foreign Affairs, have taken a personal share
in the conception, preparation and drafting of the new Pact.

We owe special thanks to those who have undergone the
fatigue of a long journey in order to be present at this manifestation.

I have no doubt that you are all ready to join me in the
same grateful impulse to one of our colleagues who did not
hesitate to come himself and assert here, with the full moral
authority attached to his name and the great country which
he represents, his steady faith in the importance and scope of
the deed which we are about to sign. Sitting to-day amongst
us, in this very hall where his illustrious forerunner, President

Wilson, had already brought to the work of peace such a high conscience of the part played by his country, the Hon. Mr. Kellogg can look back with just feelings of pride on the progress that has been made, in such a short time, since the day when we both began to examine the means of carrying out this far-reaching diplomatic undertaking. Nobody was better qualified than he to play in the negotiations that have been brought to a successful issue the prominent part that is his due and which will ever redound to his credit in the memory of men. Optimistic and tenacious as he is, he has got the better of sceptics; his entire fairness and good faith, the readiness with which he satisfied legitimate queries by clear and definite explanations, gained him the confidence of all his partners; and lastly, it was his clear vision that showed him what can be expected of Governments inspired by the deep yearnings of nations.

What more exalted lesson could be offered to the civilized world than the sight of an assembly in which, for the signing of a Pact against War, Germany, of her own free will, steps in on a level with all and takes her seat amongst other signatories, her former adversaries? The example is still more strikingly illustrated when an opportunity is thus given to a representative of France, receiving, for the first time since more than half a century, a German Foreign Minister on French soil, to extend to him the same welcome as to all his foreign colleagues. Let me add, gentlemen, that when this delegate of Germany is called Herr Stresemann, I can be believed to be particularly glad to pay due homage to the distinguished mind and the courage of the eminent statesman who has not hesitated to assume for more than three years full responsibility in the work of European co-operation for the maintenance of peace.

Since I have been so far as to mention names, you will not take it amiss, and certainly Lord Cushendun will approve me, if I personally evoke amongst us, with a brotherly feeling, the name of Sir Austen Chamberlain. Allow me to address him all our wishes of speedy and full return to health. When I think of the unwearying devotion that the cause of peace has always fostered in his noble soul, I cannot help imagining the joy which so determined an enemy of war would have felt at the sight of a meeting such as this. As to ourselves, we must perforce believe he is still with us, whether invisible or in the flesh, at any manifestation of peace.

. . . . . .

It will be, I hope, no exaggeration to say that to-day's event marks a new date in the history of mankind.

For the first time, on a general plane, accessible to all the nations of the universe, a congress of peace does something else than settle politically the immediate conditions of a particular peace, such as they are imposed, in fact, by the results of war. For the first time, on a comprehensive and absolute scale, a treaty is truly devoted to the very establishment of peace, initiating a new law, and freed from all political contingencies. Such a treaty is a beginning and not an end unto itself.

Nor have we met to liquidate a war. The Pact of Paris, born of peace, and drawn from a free juridical notion, can and must be a regular treaty of concord. That is no doubt why Mr. Kellogg, when he insisted on leaving to the French Government the privilege of receiving you in Paris, was so kind as to tell the French Ambassador it seemed to him quite fitting that the neighbourhood of the Place de la Concorde should be chosen for signing the Pact.

The Treaties of Locarno, after the Dawes Plan, had already borne witness to this new spirit that now finds its full vent. All their signatories were quite familiar with the idea of renunciation of war as an instrument of national policy, as I had the occasion of saying in my message to the American people on April 6, 1927. But those practical agreements, calculated to create a political guarantee of peace in a definite section of Europe, could not, because of their very nature, assume that universal character from which the General Pact against War derives all its value.

The League of Nations, deeply imbued with the same spirit,

had likewise issued a declaration tending, in fact, to obtain eventually the same result as the new Pact. But, apart from the fact that the United States had no share in it, the formula and the methods of the League could not be the same as those to which it has been possible for us to have recourse for such a general and absolute agreement as the Pact provides. The League of Nations—a vast political undertaking of insurance against war, a powerful institution of organized peace, where there is room to welcome all fresh contributions to the common work—cannot but rejoice at the signing of an international contract whereby she is to benefit. Far from being inconsistent with any of her obligations, this new act, on the contrary, offers her a kind of general reinsurance. Thus those of her members who will soon be able to ask the League to register to-day's contract will rightly feel that they are bringing her a precious token of their attachment and loyalty.

.   .   .   .   .   .

It may now be appropriate to explain what is finally the essential feature of the Pact against War.

It is this : For the first time, in face of the whole world, through a solemn covenant, involving the honour of great nations that all have behind them a heavy past of political conflicts, war is renounced unreservedly as an instrument of national policy—that is to say, in its most specific and dreaded form : selfish and wilful war. Considered of yore as of divine right and having remained in international ethics as an attribute of sovereignty, that form of war becomes at last juridically devoid of what constituted its most serious danger : its legitimacy. Henceforth branded with illegality, it is by mutual accord truly and regularly outlawed, so that the culprit would incur the unconditional condemnation and probably the enmity of all the co-signatories. It is a direct blow to the institution of war, even to its very vitals. It is no longer a question of a defensive organization against the scourge, but of attacking the evil at the root itself.

Thus shall war, as a means of arbitrary and selfish action, no longer be deemed lawful. Thus its threat shall no longer hang over the economic, political and social life of the peoples. Thus shall the smaller nations henceforth enjoy real independence in international discussions. Freed from the old bondage, the nations that have signed the new contract will gradually forsake the habit of associating the idea of national prestige and national interest with the idea of force. And this single psychological fact will not be the least important factor in the evolution that is needed to lead to a regular stabilization of peace.

Oh, but this is not realism, it has been said. And are not sanctions lacking? It might be asked whether true realism consists in excluding from the realm of facts the moral forces, amongst which is that of public opinion. In effect, the State which would act so as to incur the reprobation of all its partners would run the positive risk of seeing all of them gradually and freely gather against it, with the redoubtable consequences that would not be long to ensue. And where is the country, signatory to the Pact, that its leaders would, on their own responsibility, expose to such a danger? The modern law of interdependence between the nations makes it incumbent upon every statesman to take up for himself these memorable words of President Coolidge: "An act of war, in any part of the world, is an act that injures the interests of my country."

Now we can realize how important it is to extend the scope of this wide ring of international solidarity, which tends, as to an ideal end, to encompass the whole of the universe.

When on June 20, 1927, I had the honour of proposing to the Hon. Mr. Kellogg the form of words which he decided to accept and embody in the draft of a multi-lateral Pact, I never contemplated for one moment that the suggested engagement should only exist between France and the United States—indeed, I have always thought that, in one way or another, through multiplication or extension, the proposed Covenant would in itself possess an expanding force, strong enough to reach rapidly all the nations whose moral adhesion was indispensable. It was, therefore, a source of gratification to me to see Mr. Kellogg, from the beginning of the active negotiations that he was to lead with such a clear-sighted and persevering mind, advocate the extension of the Pact, and assign to it that universal character that fully answered the wishes of the French Government.

It may be said that this desirable universality, that was at the origin of the Pact, has already found its application in actual practice, for the intentions expressed by many Governments enable us even now to consider the spiritual community of nations that are morally represented at this first signature, as being much wider than it appears to the onlookers. All those peoples whose delegates have not been in a position to sit amongst us to-day must realize, in this hour of complete union, our unanimous regret that for purely technical reasons it was found imperative to adopt the procedure best calculated to ensure and expedite, for the benefit of all, the success of the great undertaking. Thus the mind's eye broadens the solemn assembly of the first signatories to the General Pact for the Renunciation of War, and extends it beyond the walls of this room, even over all frontiers, whether on land or on sea. With this wide communion of men which we feel surrounding us, we are sincerely entitled to reckon that we are more than fourteen round this table. And well may you have noticed that the Government of the Republic has purposely ordered that the flags of all the nations should be hoisted over the building which is sheltering us to-day.

Gentlemen, in a moment the awakening of a great hope will be signalled to the world along the wires. It will henceforth behove us as a sacred duty to do all that can and must be done for that hope not to be disappointed. Peace is proclaimed —it is well; it is much—but it still remains necessary to organize it. In the solution of difficulties, right and not might must prevail. That is to be the work of to-morrow.

At this unforgettable hour, the conscience of the peoples, pure and rid of any national selfishness, is sincerely endeavouring to attain those serene regions where human brotherhood can be felt in the beatings of one and the same heart. Let us seek a common idea within which we can all merge our fervent hope and give up any selfish thoughts. As there is not one of the nations represented here but has shed the blood of her children on the battlefields of the last war, I propose that we should dedicate to the dead, to all the dead of the Great War, the event which we are going to consecrate together by our signature.

XL

COPY OF THE CIRCULAR NOTE PRESENTED BY THE U.S.
DIPLOMATIC REPRESENTATIVES TO THE NATIONS NOT
SIGNATORY TO THE PEACE PACT, INVITING THE
ADHERENCE OF THEIR GOVERNMENTS TO THE PACT

August 27th, 1928.

YOUR EXCELLENCY,

I have the honour to inform you that the Governments
of Australia, Belgium, Canada, Czecho-Slovakia, France, Germany, Great Britain, India, the Irish Free State, Italy, Japan,
New Zealand, Poland, South Africa, and the United States
of America have this day signed in Paris a Treaty binding
them to renounce war as an instrument of national policy in
their relations with one another, and to seek only by pacific
means the settlement or solution of all disputes which may
arise among them.

This Treaty, as Your Excellency is aware, is the outcome
of negotiations which commenced on June 20, 1927, when
M. Briand, Minister for Foreign Affairs of the French Republic,
submitted to my Government a draft of a pact of perpetual
friendship between France and the United States. In the course
of the subsequent negotiations this idea was extended so as
to include as original signatories of the anti-war treaty not
only France and the United States, but also Japan, the British
Empire, and all the Governments which participated with
France and Great Britain in the Locarno Agreements, namely,
Belgium, Czecho-Slovakia, Germany, Italy, and Poland. This
procedure met the point raised by the British Government in
its Note of May 19, 1928, where it stated that the Treaty from
its very nature was not one which concerned that Government
alone, but was one in which that Government could not undertake to participate otherwise than jointly and simultaneously
with the Governments in the Dominions and the Government
of India; it also settled satisfactorily the question whether
there was any inconsistency between the new Treaty and the
Treaties of Locarno, thus meeting the observations of the

French Government as to the necessity of extending the number of original signatories.

The decision to limit the original signatories to the Powers named above—that is, to the United States, Japan, the parties to the Locarno Treaties, the British Dominions, and India—was based entirely upon practical considerations. It was the desire of the United States that negotiations be successfully concluded at the earliest possible moment, and that the Treaty become operative without the delay that would inevitably result were prior universal acceptance made a condition precedent to its coming into force. My Government felt, moreover, that if these Powers could agree upon a simple renunciation of war as an instrument of national policy there could be no doubt that most, if not all, of the other Powers of the world would find the formula equally acceptable and would hasten to lend their unqualified support to so impressive a movement for the perpetuation of peace. The United States has, however, been anxious from the beginning that no State should feel deprived of an opportunity to participate promptly in the new Treaty, and thus not only align itself formally and solemnly with this new manifestation of the popular demand for world peace, but also avail itself of the identical benefits enjoyed by the original signatories. Accordingly, in the draft treaty proposed by it, the United States made specific provision for participation in the treaty by any and every Power desiring to identify itself therewith, and this same provision is found in the definitive instrument signed to-day in Paris It will also be observed that the Powers signing the Treaty have recorded in the preamble their hope that every nation of the world will participate in the Treaty, and in that connection I am happy to be able to say that my Government has already received from several Governments informal indications that they are prepared to do so at the earliest possible moment. This convincing evidence of the world-wide interest and sympathy which the new Treaty has evoked is most gratifying to all the Governments concerned.

In these circumstances I have the honour formally to

communicate to Your Excellency for your consideration and for the approval of your Government, if it concurs therein, the text of the above-mentioned Treaty as signed to-day in Paris, omitting only that part of the preamble which names the several plenipotentiaries. [The text follows (see page 188).]

The provisions regarding ratification and adherence are, as Your Excellency will observe, found in the third and last article. That article provides that the Treaty shall take effect as soon as the ratifications of all the Powers named in the preamble shall have been deposited in Washington, and that it shall be open to adherence by all the other Powers of the world, instruments evidencing such adherence to be deposited in Washington also. Any Power desiring to participate in the Treaty may thus exercise the right to adhere thereto, and my Government will be happy to receive at any time appropriate notices of adherence from those Governments wishing to contribute to the success of this new movement for world peace by bringing their peoples within its beneficent scope. It will be noted in this connection that the Treaty expressly provides that when it has come into force it shall take effect immediately between an adhering Power and the other parties thereto, and it is therefore clear that any Government adhering promptly will fully share in the benefits of the Treaty at the very moment it comes into effect.

I shall shortly transmit for Your Excellency's convenient reference a printed pamphlet containing the text in translation of M. Briand's original proposal to my Government of June 20, 1927, and the complete record of the subsequent diplomatic correspondence on the subject of a multi-lateral treaty for the renunciation of war. I shall also transmit as soon as received from my Government a certified copy of the signed Treaty.

XLI

NOTE OF THE SOVIET GOVERNMENT CONTAINING ITS ADHESION TO THE PEACE PACT

Moscow,
August 31, 1928.

HIS EXCELLENCY
THE FRENCH AMBASSADOR,
THE FRENCH EMBASSY,
MOSCOW.

YOUR EXCELLENCY,

You were kind enough to inform me on August 27, 1928, on the order of your Government, that on that day the Governments of the German Republic, of Belgium, France, Great Britain and her Dominions, Italy, Japan, Poland, and Czecho-Slovakia, signed at Paris the multi-lateral Pact, by which they bind themselves not to have recourse, in their mutual relations, to war as an instrument of their national policy, but to seek the solution of the disputes which may arise between them by none but pacific means.

In your Note, enclosing the copy of the text of the Pact and describing its history, you were also kind enough to inform me that the limitation of the numbers of the original signatories was due solely, as the Government of the United States declares, to purely practical considerations, with a view to facilitating the effective application of the Pact with the shortest possible delay, but that the intention had always been to throw the Pact open to all the nations of the world, on the same conditions and with the same advantages as those accorded to the original signatories, as soon as the project of the Pact had been definitely realized; that the Government of the United States was henceforth ready to receive the instruments of adhesion to the Pact of the Governments of those nations; that the Government of the French Republic had undertaken to communicate to the Government of the Soviet Union, through Your Excellency, the text of the above-mentioned Pact, and to ask whether it was prepared to accede to it, and, if such were the case, that Your Excellency was authorized to receive, for transmission to Washington, the instrument of the adhesion of my Government to the Pact.

In communicating to you, by this Note, the reply of the Government of the Soviet Union to your invitation, I have the honour to request you to communicate the following observations to your Government, and to be kind enough to transmit them to the Government of the United States :—

1. Having taken, from the very beginning of its existence, as the basis of its foreign policy, the preservation and security of world peace, the Soviet Government always and everywhere acted as a constant adherent to peace, and went half-way to meet every step in the direction of peace. At the same time the Soviet Government considered, and still considers, that the carrying out of a plan of universal and complete disarmament is the only practical means of preventing armed conflicts, because in an atmosphere of general feverish armament all competition amongst the Powers inevitably leads to war, which is the more destructive in proportion to the state of perfection of the system of armaments. A project of complete disarmament was worked out in detail and proposed by the delegation of the Soviet Union to the Preparatory Commission for the Disarmament Conference at Geneva, but unfortunately it did not find support from the majority of the Commission, that majority including the representatives of those Powers which are the original signatories of the Pact signed in Paris. The project was declined notwithstanding the fact that its acceptance and realization would have meant a real guarantee of peace.

2. Not wishing to neglect any opportunity of contributing to the reduction of the burden of armaments, borne by the masses of the people, the Soviet Government, after the rejection of its proposals for complete disarmament, not only did not decline to discuss the question of a partial decrease of armaments, but, through its delegation on the Preparatory Commission, itself came forward with a scheme of partial but effective disarmament, also worked out in detail. The Soviet

Government must regretfully state that this scheme also failed to meet with sympathy on the Preparatory Commission, whose action demonstrated once afresh the weakness of the League of Nations in the cause of disarmament—the strongest guarantee of peace and the most potent method of abolishing war—by the rejection of the Soviet proposals by almost all the States who have now given their signatures to the Pact renouncing war.

3. Besides its systematic defence of the cause of disarmament long before the idea of the newly signed Paris Pact was conceived, the Soviet Government addressed to the other Powers a proposal for the renunciation of war through the conclusion of bi-lateral Pacts. That proposal aimed not only at the kind of warfare stigmatized by the Paris Pact, but also at any attack by one State on another, and, indeed, at any armed conflict whatsoever. Some States, such as Germany, Turkey, Afghanistan, Persia, and Lithuania, accepted the proposal and concluded Pacts with the Soviet Government. Other States silently ignored the proposal, making the strange explanation that unconditional renunciation of aggression was incompatible with their obligations towards the League of Nations. Those considerations did not, however, prevent those very Powers from signing the Paris Pact, whose text is silent as to the inviolability of such obligations.

4. These facts are irrefutable proof that the idea of the renunciation of war and armed conflict as an instrument of national policy is the basis and leading idea of Soviet foreign policy. Nevertheless, the initiators of the Paris Pact did not deem it necessary to invite the Soviet Government to take part in the negotiations leading up to the Pact or in the drafting of the text. Moreover, those Powers which were indeed interested in the guaranteeing of peace, either as having been the objects of attack (such as Turkey and Afghanistan), or as being now the objects of attack (such as the Republic of the great Chinese people), were also not invited. Furthermore, the invitation for adherence to the Paris Pact transmitted through the French Government does not mention any conditions

which would permit the Soviet Government to secure any modifications in the text. The Soviet Government postulates as an axiom that under no conditions can it consent to being deprived of that right which the other signatory Governments had or could have had, and on the basis of that axiom it must first make several observations as to its attitude towards the Pact itself.

5. First of all, the Soviet Government cannot refrain from expressing its deepest regret at the absence in the Paris Pact of any obligations whatever as regards disarmament. The Soviet delegation to the Preparatory Commission has already had the opportunity of declaring that only an anti-war Pact providing for complete and universal disarmament can be really effective in guaranteeing universal peace, and that, on the contrary, any international treaty "forbidding war" but unaccompanied by even such an elementary guarantee as the limitation of incessantly growing armaments cannot but remain a dead letter. The recent public statements of some of the signatories of the Paris Pact that further armaments are inevitable, even after its conclusion, confirm the Soviet attitude. The new international political groups which have made their appearance at the same time, especially in connection with the question of naval armaments, emphasize this situation. The conditions created by these events point now more than ever before to the necessity of resolute measures in the domain of disarmament.

6. As regards the text of the Pact, the Soviet Government deems it necessary to point out that there is not enough precision or clarity in the first clause as regards the very formula for the prohibition of wars, which permits various and arbitrary interpretations. It believes that any war must be forbidden, whether as an instrument of so-called "national policy" or for any other purpose (such as the oppression of national liberation movements). In the opinion of the Soviet Government there must be a ban not only on war in its formal juridical sense (such as normally follows a declaration of war), but also such military actions as a blockade or the occupation

of foreign territory, etc. The history of recent years has furnished several examples of such military activities, which have inflicted terrible hardships on the peoples. The Soviet Republics themselves were the object of such attacks, and now 400,000,000 Chinese are suffering similarly. Such military actions often grow into big wars, which it may be impossible absolutely to prevent. Meanwhile these questions—very important as they are from the point of view of the preservation of peace—are passed over in silence.

To revert to Clause 1 of the Pact, this speaks of the necessity of solving all international disputes and conflicts exclusively by peaceful means. As regards this the Soviet Government considers that amongst the non-peaceful means forbidden by the Pact must be included such means as a refusal to re-establish peaceful normal relations or the rupture of such relations between peoples. Such actions mean the suspension of peaceful methods for the solution of disputes, and the consequent exacerbation of relations contributes to the creation of an atmosphere favourable to the outbreak of war.

7. Amongst the reservations made in the course of the preliminary diplomatic correspondence between the original participants the especial attention of the Soviet Government has been evoked by the British reservation in paragraph 10 of its Note of May 19th of this year, whereby the British Government reserves its freedom of action as regards a series of regions not specifically mentioned. If this reservation is meant to refer to regions already belonging to the British Empire or its Dominions, it is apparently superfluous, since they are already included in the Pact, and the possibility of their being attacked is provided for in it. If, however, some other regions are meant, the participants of the Pact are entitled to know exactly where the freedom of action of the British Government begins and ends.

But the British Government reserves its freedom of action not only in the case of military attack on those regions, but also in the case of "an unfriendly" act or so-called "interference," while it obviously reserves the right to an arbitrary definition of what is to be considered as "an unfriendly act" or "interference" which would justify military action on its part. The recognition of such a right as is claimed by the British Government would mean the justification of war, and might be an example for other nations to follow who by virtue of equality of status would take advantage of the same right. The probable result would be that there would not be a single spot in the world where the terms of the Pact were applicable. Indeed, the British reservation contains an invitation to another participant in the Pact to exempt it from the provisions of the Pact in regard to other regions. The Soviet Government cannot help regarding this reservation as an attempt to use the Pact itself as an instrument of imperialistic policy.

However, the British Government's Note referred to has not been communicated to the Soviet Government as being an integral part of the Pact or its annexes, and therefore cannot be considered as binding on the Soviet Government any more than any other of the reservations mentioned in the diplomatic correspondence about the Pact amongst the original participants. Moreover, the Soviet Government cannot consent to any other reservations which might be calculated to serve as justification for war, particularly reservations made in the correspondence designed to exempt from the application of the Pact obligations ensuing from the Covenant of the League of Nations and the Locarno Agreement.

Summarizing what I have said above, I must again emphasize the absence in the Pact of obligations to disarm—the only essential element for the guaranteeing of peace, the inadequacy and lack of precision of the very formula for the prohibition of war, and the existence of several reservations having the object in advance of suspending any appearance of obligation towards the cause of peace. Nevertheless, inasmuch as the Paris Pact objectively imposes certain obligations on the Powers before world opinion, and gives the Soviet Government another opportunity to bring once again to the attention of the participants in the Pact the most important factor for peace—the question of disarmament, the solution of which is the only guarantee for the prevention of war—the Soviet Government expresses its readiness to sign the Paris Pact.

In pursuance of this decision, I shall have the honour to hand over to you, M. l'Ambassadeur, the act of my Government adhering to the Pact as soon as the formalities in connection with it are concluded.

Accept, etc.,

(*Signed*)   LITVINOV.

XLII

TEXT OF THE TREATY

The following is the English text of the Treaty:—

The President of the United States of America, the President of the French Republic, His Majesty the King of the Belgians, the President of the Czecho-Slovak Republic, His Majesty the King of Great Britain, Ireland, and the British Dominions beyond the Seas, Emperor of India, the President of the German Reich, His Majesty the King of Italy, His Majesty the Emperor of Japan, the President of the Republic of Poland,

Deeply sensible of their solemn duty to promote the welfare of mankind; persuaded that the time has come when a frank renunciation of war as an instrument of national policy should be made, to the end that the peaceful and friendly relations now existing between their peoples may be perpetuated;

Convinced that all changes in their relations with one another should be sought only by pacific means and be the result of a peaceful and orderly process, and that any signatory Power which shall hereafter seek to promote its national interests by resort to war should be denied the benefits furnished by this Treaty;

Hopeful that, encouraged by their example, all the other nations of the world will join in this humane endeavour and, by adhering to the present Treaty as soon as it comes into force, bring their peoples within the scope of its beneficent provisions, thus uniting the civilized nations of the world in a common renunciation of war as an instrument of their national policy;

Have decided to conclude a treaty, and for that purpose have appointed as their respective plenipotentiaries: . . . Who, having communicated to one another their full powers, found in good and due form, have agreed upon the following articles:—

ARTICLE I.—The High Contracting Parties solemnly declare,

in the names of their respective peoples, that they condemn recourse to war for the solution of international controversies, and renounce it as an instrument of national policy in their relations with one another.

ARTICLE II.—The High Contracting Parties agree that the settlement or solution of all disputes or conflicts, of whatever nature or of whatever origin they may be, which may arise among them, shall never be sought except by pacific means.

ARTICLE III.—The present Treaty shall be ratified by the High Contracting Parties named in the preamble in accordance with their respective constitutional requirements, and shall take effect as between them as soon as all their several instruments of ratification shall have been deposited at Washington.

This Treaty shall, when it has come into effect as prescribed in the preceding paragraph, remain open as long as may be necessary for adherence by all the other Powers of the world. Every instrument evidencing the adherence of a Power shall be deposited at Washington, and the Treaty shall, immediately upon such deposit, become effective as between the Power thus adhering and the other Powers parties thereto.

It shall be the duty of the Government of the U.S.A. to furnish each Government named in the preamble, and every Government subsequently adhering to this Treaty, with a certified copy of the Treaty, and of every instrument of ratification or adherence. It shall also be the duty of the Government of the U.S.A. telegraphically to notify such Governments immediately upon the deposit with it of each instrument of ratification or adherence.

In faith whereof the respective plenipotentiaries have signed this Treaty in the French and English languages, both texts having equal force, and hereunto affixed their seals.

Done at Paris, the twenty-seventh day of August, in the Year of Our Lord one thousand nine hundred and twenty-eight.

APPENDIX A

PRINCIPAL FIGURES IN THE PEACE PACT NEGOTIATIONS

In Washington.

The Hon. Frank B. Kellogg	Secretary of State.
The Hon. William S. Borah	Chairman of the Foreign Relations Committee of the Senate.
Right Hon. Sir Esmé Howard	British Ambassador.
M. Paul Claudel	French Ambassador.
Dr. F. W. von Prittwitz und Graffon	German Ambassador.
Cav. Giacomo de Martino	Italian Ambassador.
Mr. Tsunco Matsudaira	Japanese Ambassador.
Hon. Vincent Massey	Canadian Minister.
Professor Timothy A. Smiddy	Minister of the Irish Free State.
Prince Albert de Ligne	Belgian Ambassador.
Herr Zdenek Fierlinger	Czecho-Slovak Minister.
M. Jan Ciechanowski	Polish Minister.

In London.

Right Hon. Sir Austen Chamberlain, K.G.	Secretary of State for Foreign Affairs.
Hon. Alanson B. Houghton	American Ambassador.
Mr. Ray Atherton	American Chargé d'Affaires.
M. de Fleuriau	French Ambassador.

In Ottawa.

Right Hon. William Mackenzie King	Prime Minister and Minister for External Affairs.
Hon. William Philips	American Minister.

In Dublin.

Mr. Patrick McGilligan	Minister for External Affairs.
Hon. Frederick A. Sterling	American Minister.

In Paris.

M. Aristide Briand	Minister for Foreign Affairs.
Hon. Myron T. Herrick	American Ambassador.

In Berlin.

Dr. Gustav Stresemann	Minister for Foreign Affairs.
Hon. Jacob G. Schurman	American Ambassador.

In Rome.

Signor Benito Mussolini . . . Prime Minister and Minister for Foreign Affairs.

Hon. Henry P. Fletcher . . . American Ambassador.

In Tokio.

Major-General Baron Tanaka . . Prime Minister and Minister for Foreign Affairs.

Hon. Charles MacVeagh . . . American Ambassador.

In Brussels.

M. Paul Hymans . . . . . Minister for Foreign Affairs.

Hon. Hugh S. Gibson . . . . American Ambassador.

In Prague.

Dr. Edward Beneš . . . . Minister for Foreign Affairs.

Hon. Lewis Einstein . . . . American Ambassador.

In Warsaw.

M. A. Zalewski . . . . . Minister for Foreign Affairs.

Hon. John B. Stetson, Jr. . . . American Minister.

In Madrid.

General Primo de Riviera, Marques Prime Minister and Minister
de Estella . . . . . . for Foreign Affairs.

Hon. Ogden Hammond . . . American Ambassador.

APPENDIX B

LIST OF STATES WHICH HAVE ADHERED TO THE PACT

BOLIVIA, BRAZIL, AUSTRIA, DENMARK, CUBA, LIBERIA, PERU AND RUMANIA	August 29, 1928
LUXEMBURG AND GREECE	August 30, 1928
SWITZERLAND, FINLAND, THE NETHERLANDS, PANAMA AND URUGUAY	August 31, 1928
ESTHONIA	September 3, 1928
ABYSSINIA, EGYPT,[1] PORTUGAL, VENEZUELA AND SWEDEN	September 4, 1928
CHINA, LITHUANIA AND THE U.S.S.R.[2]	September 6, 1928
TURKEY AND THE ARGENTINE[3]	September 8, 1928
SPAIN	September 11, 1928
MEXICO	September 15, 1920
PERSIA[4]	September 17, 1928
BULGARIA[5]	October 2, 1928
HUNGARY	October 8, 1928

[1] Adherence not to be considered as the acceptance of any reservations made concerning it by any Powers.

[2] The Presidium of the Soviet Executive Committee authorized Soviet adhesion to the Pact on August 29th. The formal adhesion of the Soviet Government was received by the State Department in Washington, through the French Embassy, on October 4, 1928.

[3] The Senate adopted a resolution endorsing the Pact on September 8th.

[4] The Special Committee appointed by the Government to consider the Pact recommended that the Government should sign it, but with the proviso that it did not adhere to the conditions and reservations made by certain European Governments.

The State Department in Washington announced on October 5th that it had received a notification from the Persian Government of its intention to sign the Pact.

[5] It was learnt in Sofia on October 2nd that the Minister for Foreign Affairs had authorized the Bulgarian Minister in Washington to sign the Pact.

RATIFICATIONS OF THE PACT

It was announced by the State Department in Washington on September 12th that by that date Peru, Liberia, and Rumania had "officially adhered to the Pact of Peace." In addition, Bolivia announced its formal adherence on October 12, 1928. Latvia, Honduras, Haiti, Yugoslavia, Costa Rica and the Dominican Republic had also signified their intention of adhering.